PRAISE FOR

A note from Lindsay: Each time a book is written, the author is responsible for finding people to read their book before it's released and then endorse the book as a sort of social proof that the book is worth the read. It makes sense that the normal course of action is to find the people with the largest following or the most clout behind their reputation to write the endorsements. But what does a semi-famous person who doesn't really know me, my story, or my book have to say that the people in my life who have already been affected by this book can't? The answer is nothing.

I want you to hear endorsements from people who know me, have worked with me, or have actually been affected by the words I wrote in this book. For that reason, I didn't reach out to the most successful people I have connected with during my writing career to endorse *Wake Up!* Instead, I reached out to people, just like you and me, who have come into my life for a reason and understand this content on a very personal level. You're about to read endorsements from some of my friends, coworkers, mentors, neighbors, and even my previous employees.

Wake Up! is a personal book, written in a personal way; it only makes sense that you would take the word of those who have witnessed this book's words in a very personal way.

"My eyes were filled with awe and wonder as I witnessed Lindsay's *Wake Up!* process in real-time. Observing the energy and excitement of a life reborn was contagious. Having the opportunity to enter into this process personally through this book was a powerful experience. Lindsay's gift of asking inspiring and thought-provoking questions shined through like a powerful beacon of light that revealed my next steps forward into creating a life I love living. This book guides you through the powerful journey of fully stepping into your story, consciously grabbing the pen, and writing the best chapter yet in the story of your life."

ROSY CRESCITELLI (HUMAN DESIGN SPECIALIST)
RELATIONSHIP: LINDSAY'S FRIEND + COWORKER

"Wow. *Wake Up!* is a miracle to me. What Lindsay has figured out and then made into this book is nothing short of the work of the Holy Spirit and someone fiercely dedicated to following His voice. This said, I believe this book is groundbreaking for the church. As dramatic as that may sound, in *Wake Up!*, Lindsay bravely, wisely, and powerfully uncovers a way that has been lost on us for too long. You'll finish the last page—or even the third chapter—and want to thank her profusely for her toil in writing this for you. For us all! This book will resonate with your soul as the deepest truth and will simply change your life. Open your heart, open your mind, dig in, then do everything she says. You'll be so glad you did!"

KATIE MOON (BIBLICAL RESEARCHER + COURSE CREATOR)
RELATIONSHIP: INTERNET FRIENDS, TECHNICALLY, BUT SOUL SISTERS
AND EACH OTHER'S SPIRIT ANIMALS, NON-TECHNICALLY

"I was not only there when Lindsay was writing *Wake Up!*, but I have lived this content for the last three years, and it has changed me as I watched it change her. At first, I was going along to support her vision for this book, but in the end, I was the beneficiary of all the lessons I learned along the way. I'm now a more authentic and capable husband, father, and human being. My relationship with everything in my life is changed because I learned how to change it. *Wake Up!* is about to shake everything up for you, and Lindsay is the perfect person to present this to the world. I'm never going back to sleep, and nobody can make me!"

MICHAEL MORENO (CFO, FATHER + HUSBAND)
RELATIONSHIP: LINDSAY'S HUSBAND + BIGGEST FAN

"Lindsay came with this book in the middle of what felt like the world falling to pieces. *Wake Up!* didn't just startle me out of my deep sleep; it nudged me into a slow and steady rising to living the life I'm here for. The rapid, real, and tangible successes that have come from my consumption and application of these pages are illimitable."

YOSHIKA GREEN (WRITER, EDITOR + CONSULTANT)
RELATIONSHIP: I'M THE FRIEND WHO SAW LINDSAY IN A LARGE, CROWDED
ROOM AND DANCED RIGHT OVER TO HER, *SOUL TRAIN*-STYLE, THE FIRST TIME
WE MET. OUR COLLECTIVE ENERGY WAS MAGNETIZING FROM THE START.
WE'VE BEEN CLOSE EVER SINCE, DESPITE GEOGRAPHICAL DISTANCE.

"Oops, she did it again! LTM is the master of gathering information, creating replicable ideas, and breaking them down so you not only actually understand these big ideas but are able to implement them and succeed. *Wake Up!* will shake you up and give you the tools to really start living that good life. #freebritney"

CARRIE HOENER (NONPROFIT COFOUNDER OF RE:JOYCE)
RELATIONSHIP: THE QUIET FRIEND—UNTIL YOU LET HER DRESS
UP LIKE WILL FARRELL AT A MOVIE-THEMED PARTY

"I could write a lot about what *Wake Up!* made me feel, but that kind of public vulnerability is something I leave to Lindsay. The challenges in this book have changed me, and the push for more in my life has set me on a path I didn't know existed. I follow Lindsay's advice because I've seen the changes in her firsthand. That's the kind of thing this book will do to a community. Once you read it, nobody that knows you is safe. You've been warned!"

LEAH FRIEDMAN (BUSINESS OWNER + SOCIAL BUTTERFLY)
RELATIONSHIP: LINDSAY'S FRIEND + COWORKER

"Honestly, this book had me at 'let's get our morbid on for a minute.' *Wake Up!* is full of humor, perspective, gut checks, and questions that really make you feel the urgency to take action like your life depends on it because—guess what—it does. If the last year and a half has taught us anything, let it be that we no longer have time to waste. We deserve to live a fulfilled, purposeful, and passionate life *now*. *Wake Up!* is the map to the buried treasure. The gold is there; you just have to be willing to dig to uncover it. Lindsay will guide you toward the X. I hope you brought your shovel. Happy digging!"

MALISSA HAMIDY (CERTIFIED LIFE COACH + TACO ENTHUSIAST)
RELATIONSHIP: LINDSAY'S FRIEND + COWORKER + FELLOW SUN DEVIL

"*Wake Up!* is the most honest and valuable book you'll read this year. If you're ready to admit you've been sleeping through life, as most of us have, this book is for you. From vulnerable stories to years of research to successful practice, *Wake Up!* has everything you need to change your life if you let it."

ELIZABETH BIENAS (OPERATIONS ADVISOR, COPYWRITER, INVESTOR)
RELATIONSHIP: THE YIN TO LINDSAY'S BUSINESS YANG FOR THE LAST DECADE

"*Wake Up!* is a dangerous book, and it will change you. Lindsay powerfully breaks down the constructs of success and balance that have permeated our modern lives and reignites a childlike wonder, meaning, purpose, and love for life that rocks you to your very core. Be warned: the 'you' that starts this book will not be the same 'you' that finishes it—and you will *love it*."

DEREK VONIGAS (ARMCHAIR THEOLOGIAN AND SELF-PROCLAIMED KING OF NERDS)
RELATIONSHIP: FELLOW BOOK ADDICT AND FRIEND FOR MANY AN AGE

"*Wake Up!* spoke to me. I was reminded of events in my life and how I was the only one holding myself back. LTM deep dives not only into her own vulnerable experiences but gives you a guideline on how to move past them, love yourself, and live the life you deserve."

ANNI DAYAN (CAREGIVER + REALTOR)
RELATIONSHIP: I MET LINDSAY AT WORK, AND WITHIN MOMENTS I
FELT A CONNECTION THAT SAID, "WE'VE BEEN HERE BEFORE." EVER
MET SOMEONE AND CONNECTED LIKE THAT? IT'S MAGIC.

"*Wake Up!* brought me to action, to change, and to the realization that I can be a better mom, wife, friend, etc. *now*. This book is uncomfortable and challenging in the best way. These words will move you!"

LINDSAY BIGGS (TINY HUMAN MOM)
RELATIONSHIP: FRIEND + PAST ASSISTANT + CHRISTMAS
OBSESSION DECORATING PARTNER

"*Wake Up!* is a refreshing view at taking a hard look at how you think and react to situations to move you forward in your life. Not only does Lindsay talk about what's happening in your head, but she also gives tools on how to combat negative thoughts. A great read for anyone needing help getting unstuck with negativity."

MELISSA KOEHLER (FOUNDER OF THE BLUSH PAGES)
RELATIONSHIP: LINDSAY'S FRIEND + COWORKER + TRAVEL BUDDY

"Every time LTM puts pen to paper, she blows me away with her wit, wisdom, and relevance to today's world. Her encouragement helps me feel like I am not alone one bit with the typical struggles we all face. And, of course, *Wake Up!* comes with a hefty side of laughter too."

JODIE MESCHUK (QUANTUM MEDICINE / AUTISM RECOVERY)
RELATIONSHIP: LINDSAY'S TEXTING BUDDY + FELLOW AUTHOR + ENTREPRENEUR

"Lindsay is more than an alarm clock. She's a whole intervention. *Wake Up!* is a reminder that life doesn't change if you don't change."

"*Wake Up!* brilliantly reshaped my thinking with clear ideas like the 12 universal laws and then gives practical steps to living it out. Lindsay is clear, authentic, witty, and easy to follow. Lindsay is a champion of people living out their purpose without the typical self-help fluff. *Wake Up!* is full of gritty, practical steps supported by great thought and theory, then finished up with excellent ideas for execution. Read this book. It could change everything!"

"There's no fluff in these pages. Lindsay shares these life-changing principles with realness, vulnerability, and humor in a way that makes you feel like you're having a cup of coffee with a friend. Her beautiful gift of teaching others how to get the most from life is a light you will be inspired by long after reading *Wake Up!*"

"Lindsay not only has done the research, but she has put her plan into action before ever suggesting it to anyone else. Not only will this book help you get your life right, but it is also entertaining while calling you on the carpet! Don't be afraid; now is the time to *Wake Up!*"

"Having lived through the top ten shittiest moments of my life over the last year, *Wake Up!* was what I needed. I needed someone to help me put life into perspective, someone to help me reevaluate what I want and how I want to live. Lindsay has this unsettling way of reminding me of my own power and making me *want* to do the work."

"In *Wake Up!* LTM goes to those dark and dusty recesses of your mind, sits down, turns on a flashlight, dusts off the cobwebs, and gracefully takes your hand and leads you out into the sunlight and the life you've imagined."

MARY LEIGH BROWN (BOSS WHO DOES A LOT + GETS NOTHING DONE)
RELATIONSHIP: THE FRIEND LTM DIDN'T ASK FOR AND IS NOW STUCK WITH

"Lindsay is my most honest friend! Even if it's hard, she tells me the truth. *Wake Up!* is Lindsay at her best as that truth-telling friend who is real and funny and gentle and not all at the same time. This book will have you hooked from the very beginning. Hang on for the ride you never knew you needed to be on."

TROIE BATTLES (CEO LIFE & SCIENCE PUBLISHING)
RELATIONSHIP: AS FRIENDS, LINDSAY AND I LAUGH UNTIL WE PEE
SOMETIMES. IN BUSINESS, WE DO THE SAME. THE STRUGGLE IS REAL.

"This book is Lindsay. It's brave, it's challenging, it's provoking, it asks you to dig deeper and to think differently. *Wake Up!* is all her, and as expected, it will light a fire in you."

JANELL VONIGAS (BADDEST B*TCH ON THE BLOCK)
RELATIONSHIP: SECOND-GRADE BUDDIES WHO BUILT BUSINESSES TOGETHER
AS WE RAISED POTTY-TRAINING TODDLERS AND LIVED ON CHEEZ-ITS OVER
FACETIME. WE ARE RIDE-OR-DIE. "IS THIS FRIENDSHIP? I THINK SO!"

"LTM is constantly calling her own bluffs and sharing her self-tested methods for improvement. I'm excited for *Wake Up!* and having all these discoveries in one place for my convenience."

KINDRA HALL (AUTHOR)
RELATIONSHIP: INTERNET FRIENDS WHO MET IRL

"Wow, this book has it all—genius and thought-provoking insight, clear and effective steps for application, engaging and authentic writing style, and inspiration at its finest. I don't even like to read, and I couldn't put this one down!"

NIKKI DAVIS (LAWYER TURNED SOCIAL IMPACT ENTREPRENEUR)
RELATIONSHIP: SISTER FROM ANOTHER MISTER

WAKE UP!

LINDSAY TEAGUE MORENO

W Publishing Group

An Imprint of Thomas Nelson

© 2021 LTM Consulting, LLC

Published in Nashville, Tennessee, by W Publishing, an imprint of Thomas Nelson.

Published in association with Yates & Yates, www.yates2.com.

Thomas Nelson titles may be purchased in bulk for educational, business, fundraising, or sales promotional use. For information, please email SpecialMarkets@ ThomasNelson.com.

Any internet addresses, phone numbers, or company or product information printed in this book are offered as a resource and are not intended in any way to be or to imply an endorsement by Thomas Nelson, nor does Thomas Nelson vouch for the existence, content, or services of these sites, phone numbers, companies, or products beyond the life of this book.

ISBN 978-0-7852-2447-1 (HC)
ISBN 978-0-7852-2451-8 (audiobook)
ISBN 978-0-7852-2449-5 (eBook)
ISBN 978-0-7852-2448-8 (softcover)

Library of Congress Control Number: 2021942668

Printed in the United States of America
22 23 24 25 26 LSC 10 9 8 7 6 5 4 3 2 1

For my friend, mentor, and the person in my life who has expanded my definition of love beyond what I thought possible, Anni Dayan. This book is a byproduct of your good work flowing through me and into my community. I can never repay you for how you've touched my heart, but I can honor you in this way. Thank you. I love you.

CONTENTS

I WANT TO DIE
SHORT
OF BREATH
AND FULL OF
HEART!

INTRODUCTION

I was crying when I walked into the emergency room of the hospital near my house. These weren't your average hospital tears born of pain, panic, fear, or grief. Instead, I found myself wiping the shame off of my thirty-eight-year-old face one salty tear at a time.

In my experience, tears of shame are the most painful because I know in my heart I'm the one who caused them in the first place. On that winter day, I knew the problem I was about to face was one of my own making, and I absolutely hated myself for it. Over and over I asked myself why I allowed this, and I really let myself have it as I lay on that cold, paper-covered hospital bed. *What is wrong with me? Why am I still broken?*

It turns out, if you spend your life focusing on work, finances, and raising a family, a few other should-be priorities will become so desperate for your attention you'll no longer have the choice to ignore them. And those neglected things won't be something little that you put off worrying about and will instead demand your time, money, and attention when you're least prepared to give them.

Mine came in the form of high blood pressure.

And trust me, nothing spoils your best year at work like thinking, *Hmm, will it be a stroke or a heart attack today?* As an entrepreneur, my business isn't successful if I don't, you know, work! As a mother, nothing screams failure like preventable heart problems that could leave your kids motherless—a feeling I'm acutely familiar with.

I knew this wasn't a dream. This was a wake-up call.

I left the hospital that day, went home, lay in my bed, and let the shame consume me. I let it take me down to the dark place—you know the one. The one most of us avoid at all costs. The one that hurts like hell. The one that makes you feel on the outside like you do on the inside. That low that shifts so easily from helplessness to anger and often lands on the shoulders of the people we love most in the form of lashing out, deflecting, or projection. These kinds of lows drive us to reinforce that wall of solitude around our hearts and then numb ourselves until we no longer have to feel.

I let my mind take me down the timeline of my life. Ten years, twenty years, thirty years down the road. I thought of my life as a vehicle. If I continue to travel in this direction, what will my life look like?

Where will I be?

What will I feel like?

What will I do with my time?

How will I live my life?

Will I be happy?

Will I be successful?

And most importantly, will I be fulfilled?

Have I done good with the time I've been given?

Did I fulfill my purpose here on earth?

And here's the truth: I couldn't see myself older than fifty-three years old. When I asked my mind to show me the future, it did! And it couldn't get past the age of fifty-three. This was the number. This was my mom's age when she died. Fifty-three, I saw that number and did the math. My kids would be twenty-five and twenty-three. No, that's not enough time.

I sat in that feeling for a while longer before asking myself the question that changed my whole life: If I've only got a few years left to serve my purpose and find the reason that I've been put on this earth (and I believe we all—every single one of us—have one), what will I regret in my closing few hours of life?

What will I miss?

What will I hate that I never did?

How will I have affected the lives of others?

How have I left my mark on this world?

Have I loved enough?

Did I experience enough?

Have I really lived?

And there it was. Regret. My tears of shame were attached to regret.

How many people do you know who have resigned themselves to a death filled with regret rather than a life lived on purpose?

We get caught up in what's easy, what's convenient, what's planned for us, and what's conditioned into us. We make choices without even thinking. We live each day to pass the time. We mistake thrills with happiness and live to wonder why it never lasts. We fail to realize that the hard thing really is the best thing for us. We mistake the gift of the lesson for dead-end signs. It's so easy to do because it's—wait for it—normal!

Listen to me: what is normal is not necessarily what is correct for you.

On that day, in that bed, I decided to give normal the bird and I made a plan for more. Regret is something I don't have to resign myself to. This was a lesson, not a final destination. The lesson I learned that day changed the course of my life incrementally, and the work I've done in response to this event has changed the final destination by miles. What I see at the end of my life today is not what I saw on that day. And that I did on purpose.

The years 2003, 2005, 2010, 2013, and 2018 were all years that I realized I had another gear in me. Those were the years I decided that settling for success in just a few areas wasn't good enough. These were the years I realized how many of us settle for "just okay" in our lives and call it "good."

This process of building a life you love will have many iterations. You'll find what kept you fulfilled at one time won't always be the case. We should constantly be learning from ourselves and listening to our intuition about what we pursue.

At some points in my life, I understood what I was capable of, and I found I was living below my expectations for myself. I had kept the voice of my potential quiet and obedient. Following that 2018 experience in the hospital, I began demanding more from my life in a loud voice with all the certainty I had in me. I realized there was a pattern to my life. One that would lift me up to new heights, and as I'd get used to doing life up there, something new would be revealed to me. A new mountain to climb, a new goal to reach, a new desire I never had before. Each of these experiences has changed the way I think about both my life and death.

What I have learned through all of the changes in my life translates to more than just a book I can write that will help others wake up to their life too. It's a way of living that inspires anyone who comes into contact with me to want more too. I've seen it with my own eyes; I've witnessed what one life lived on fire can do for others. It is my deepest desire to do that for you through this book. I want to be the alarm that sounds so that you are fully awake and ready to walk into your next best day. I want to spark something in you so that your fire will spread in your life, marriage, family, community, workplace, and every interaction you have with others.

But that process? It's not pretty. There's this idea that self-discovery and self-love is this perfect process that looks like a caterpillar turning into a beautiful butterfly. It more closely resembles a fire ravaging your house, with every object you think you can't lose inside, leaving a pile of ashes where you used to live.

And this is where I lose most people (but not you, because you're a badass).

In my experience, most of us are so afraid to lose what we have that we don't think about what our lives could be like if we just let it go.

What would open up to us if we let go of what we used to believe would bring us true happiness and fulfillment?

What could we experience if we held everything we have with an open hand?

What lessons could we learn through the grief of letting go of the old so we can be open and ready for the new?

Who would you become if you let your spirit lead you instead of your conditioning?

What could you experience in this world if your past hurts, regrets, and wounds didn't show up in your life every day as roadblocks, but instead showed up as gifts?

You know your potential. You know what's in you. You may not believe the voice of that potential, but it's in there. You have seen glimpses of your greatness. You know what you're capable of. I know because I talk to thousands of people just like you and me. We are so much more alike than we are different. We spend our time seeking short-term comforts over long-term fulfillment. It's not your fault. We've been conditioned to think and act like this.

I'm writing this book for you because making the choice to live consciously is not ever going to get easier. In fact, it's going to get harder and harder because being entertained and distracted from what really matters is going to get easier and easier. Don't sign me up for a world where it's acceptable to live each day just to die on a random Tuesday and say, "Welp, it was a good run, guys." No, I want us to live in a way where death has to work to do its business. I want death to chase us down the road. I want to die short of breath and full of heart.

The booming sound of the alarm that you're feeling right now as you read these words is for you. If you're willing to dance in the ashes of the old, you will open yourself to who you really are, what you're actually capable of, and what you truly want out of life. You can never do that when you're living

> I want us to live in a way where death has to work to do its business. I want death to chase us down the road.

someone else's version of happy and fulfilled. This is the right time; this is your time to really live.

You've grabbed this book because you want to do this (first "wake up" step taken). Do you hear that? It's the dawn of a new day; the rooster is crowing; it's time to wake up!

MANY OF US SETTLE FOR JUST OK IN OUR LIVES AND CALL IT GOOD

PART I

THE FOUNDATION FOR CHANGE

This is a book that's full of big ideas and challenges that could completely change your life. Not a single one of them will do you any good if you don't actually do the work laid out in each section. I've decided to lay this book out into two parts: the foundation for change and the six cornerstones of a good life. First, we're going to lay the foundation for changes that stick, and then we're going to get to work on actually changing. Along the way I'm going to tell you a few stories and give you some insight into my own life as I navigated through everything I'm about to teach you. This process scared the hell out of me, and it changed me forever. I hope the same for you, because the good life is waiting!

THERE'S NOTHING OVERNIGHT ABOUT SUCCESS

THE GOOD LIFE

I have a good life. It's a life I love. It's a life I designed through understanding who I am and what I value and then working with my physiology, psychology, and biology to make what I want for my life a reality. It's not rocket science, and you absolutely, positively can do this too.

I live a life with six distinct areas of focus, which I call the Cornerstones of a Good Life: personal, work/business, financial, health, relationship, and spiritual.

My life is not perfect. It's hard almost every day unless I seek out the easy. It is wrought with thorns in the bushes and unexpected turns in the road, but damn, it's so good. My life is filled with freedom. My life is filled with deep and profound love for myself and for others. For the most part (even with a lot of work to do on myself), I have the power and confidence to say *yes* to the opportunities that are for me and *no, thank you* to the ones that are for others. I'm not afraid of a challenge. I relish the opportunity to prove how powerful I am in the writing of my story. I refuse to settle because I don't have to. I can live in whatever way I feel called to, and I do. I change my mind a lot when I get new information. The way I live my life makes others uncomfortable at times because it cannot be controlled. You never know what I'm going to get into or discover in this wild and crazy life, and I like it like that. Some days I feel like I can fly while I watch others with the same potential and abilities continue to walk. Again, I say, we are not that different, you and me.

I don't require one hundred friends when I know a small handful will do. I don't spend my life chasing the next thrill hoping happiness lies behind it, because I already know it doesn't. I've built enough financial success to never have to work again, and yet I follow the draw toward entrepreneurship again and again. I know I sound like a self-abusive freak, but part of my purpose and fulfillment is in my work. Working toward something is where the magic lives in my life. It's afforded me so much heartbreak and failure. It's afforded me notoriety, success, and popularity, as well, which I've found isn't where fulfillment lives.

I've got a husband who has dedicated his time and energy to breaking the cycle of abuse and poverty. I've got kids who know they're loved and accepted for who they truly are. I've built a family with my husband that looks nothing like how either of us were raised. I've found a way to make my health a priority in my life despite never having the desire to take care of my own body before. I'm physically stronger and more flexible than I've ever been at forty years old. I'm now mentally stronger and more open than I've ever been.

I'm convinced I can do, create, or accomplish anything that is set before me. As long as it's going to teach me, you can bet I'm going to do it with all the vigor and dedication a human can muster. I don't half-ass anything. I go all-in with my entire mom-who-does-yoga ass. There is no second chance at this life, and I'm here to make this one a great success story.

I'm not some kind of superwoman, raised in a stress-free environment by wholehearted parents. I've hustled for every dollar in my bank account. I've fought for every relationship in my life. I've worked for every follower. I've shown up to my life through the hard stuff as an imperfect and flawed human, which has made it very clear to me that anyone can do this. Absolutely any human being has the capability to demand more from their life, and yet, at an alarming rate, we don't.

I'm going to teach you how to create that moment in your life so you can make the kinds of changes needed to feel fulfilled in all six cornerstones of your life, which I believe is the key to living and dying without regret.

I want you to believe that you can fly. You simply need to know how, and friend, that's where I shine. My playbook is open, and you're about to read it!

This same power that I have discovered in me has been discovered by so many before me, and it lays dormant in most of us. It goes unearthed, unseen, unappreciated, undiscovered, and, most unfortunate of all, unused by most people.

I'm not a genius; I'm not special; I wasn't raised with this belief, and I don't live in a way that's entirely different from the average American, except in my mind. I just had the pure audacity to believe that fulfillment exists, that I am worthy of that kind of life, and that I could find it if I tried. I'm a normal person who chose to believe that there's more and that I can make everything I want in my life real simply by deciding. One day I was in the hospital crying, and the next I put a plan in motion to never feel like that again, and as long as I continue to focus on that, I will get what I want. The same is true for you. It feels like flying.

In this book, I'm going to teach you how to fly too. You'll discover you knew you had the ability all along. You'll discover some deep truths about how powerful you've always been and that you just didn't have all the information yet to believe it or move forward through what has been keeping you stagnant. You'll discover your mind has been holding out on you in the name of safety and in avoidance of fear.

In the past decade I have systematically and strategically reevaluated and rebuilt all the parts of my life. My finances, my work, my family, my relationships, my personal desires, my health, and my spiritual relationship with my creator and the world around me are all under the microscope. Not just now, but always. Each day I learn more, think differently, become different, and therefore look for ways to change the way I live my life and act according to my values. Through this process, each step I take is met with challenge, beauty, highs, lows, wins, losses, opposition, support, backlash, discoveries, truths, lies, and every emotion on the spectrum.

It hasn't always been fun, and my ego would tell you it's cost a lot, but it's been worth it.

As I looked back at the order in which I burned my old life to the ground and the frequency with which I was willing to give it all up, I discovered patterns and paths that others either didn't see or weren't willing to explore in their own lives. I have often felt like an outsider in my life as I unearth new thoughts and ideas, and I think that simply comes from having a different mindset than my peers. I realized all the things we say that we want, like happiness and success, are down those often-overlooked paths. We get so caught up in our addictions and thrills that most of us actively reject fulfillment, having believed the lie that it is hiding behind the next exciting activity or the next positive experience. We're like addicts looking for our next hit. But our drug is dopamine, and you can get it almost anywhere you look.

We are watching, in real time, the result of a society of people who have more resources than ever before and yet are completely unsatisfied in their lives as a whole. Fulfilled humans aren't spending an average of twelve hours per day watching, listening to, reading, or interacting with the media. And yet that was the average in a 2020 Nielsen report.[1] People living a life of meaning aren't looking for ways to numb the next uncomfortable experience or feeling.

When I think about what my community (both physically and online) would be like if we were filled with whole-life fulfillment, I can see massive changes in the way we interact, live, work, play, and support one another. And I want that. I believe in the power of fulfillment. I believe individual changes trickle out like tossing a stone in a pond and watching the ripples spread outward.

The bliss we experience in our everyday lives will become ripples in the water for the people who connect with us if we're willing to wake up to our lives and realize there's more out there. I've lived it. I've seen it. I've experienced it. I want that for you. But it won't be done in the way our culture tells us it has to. We are told that it must look a certain way, it must feel a certain way, and it must all be done and changed at the same time under a false and extremely damaging idea called balance.

BALANCE

If I see one more Pinterest pin claiming to teach women the elusive but easy-to-attain secret to balance, I'm going to lose it. Let me say this plainly: balance is complete and utter bullshit. There is no such thing as balance in the good life. I rank balance right up there with the idea of a diet. In fact, I believe balance is to our fulfillment what a diet is to our health. It keeps us addicted to how others tell us we should live and keeps us controlled by products on the market that are damaging to our health and mindset in the long run, and the majority of us end up worse off than we were before we started.

I think the idea of balance is often thought to be a virtuous thing, and I often see it hanging around in articles or books that are well intentioned. Many would define balance as having a good amount of all the things we want out of life:

> I believe balance is to our fulfillment what a diet is to our health.

family, friends, work, hobbies, and whatever else we may desire. When we, as a society, first started talking about balance, our intentions were good. But over time the idea of balance has been warped into this notion of juggling all of everything all at the same time. It's not a little of everything balanced in a nice and even way. It's all of everything, piled on top of us until we're drowning in to-do lists and really cute planners with zero empty days.

If you'd like to derail your personal growth, just believe the lie that you have to do it all at once, it needs to look fun, and it needs to feel like a breath of fresh air. You'll find yourself diving face-first into in a gallon of rocky road ice cream (or whatever your preferred method of numbing is; I'm a baked goods girl, myself. Jesus be a Rice Krispies Treat with extra marshmallows and real butter. *praise hands*).

We sure do swallow whole the idea of balancing our life, don't we?

Never mind the fact we're busier than ever before and we glorify busyness as a measure of success. How is it possible that only about 9 percent of Americans say they can be both busy and happy at the same time?[2] Our culture has glorified busy because more work improves the bottom line, and we believe that happiness is hiding behind what that bottom line can provide us. We've falsely believed that money, power, status, and influence will make us happy if we just work hard enough to find them. It's designed that way to keep you asleep and keep you stuck so you stay in a predictable buying pattern. You can get off of that merry-go-round whenever you decide to, but you have to decide. You're going to decide; I can feel it.

At forty, I've had a lot of success in my career, finances, personal endeavors, and intimate relationships. Many times, I've heard people describe my path with phrases like "overnight success," and I cringe a little every time. There's nothing overnight about success. Because success isn't a thing you go get. It's a feeling you get when you evaluate your life and take action. It's an emotion you connect with when you do your work. Success isn't fifteen minutes of fame. Success isn't an event. It isn't something that blows away in the wind. Success is a mindset and series of positive habits you've diligently created and are dedicated to.

The idea of balance keeps us just out of reach of what we want. The lie that someone else has found balance keeps us searching, buying, and trying. We know we have it in us, we just have to try harder. We can do it all with a smile on, and we can provide it all without needing a rest. We can read it all, see and share it all, give it all, and hold it all together. Whole-life fulfillment will allow you to focus on your life with the freedom to lose the guilt about what you're not doing because it won't all get done at once.

This is a long-term play, not a short-term win. We're talking about creating new habits and lifestyle patterns that end up making a huge difference in your life as they become second nature to you.

This is a long-term play, not a short-term win.

WHOLE-LIFE FULFILLMENT

The only way you're going to believe that you can build a life you absolutely love with every part of your being is by discovering it. I can tell you all day, and I'll spend this entire book trying to convince you of it, but you must make the discovery yourself. You must be the one who believes there's another level out there for you. You must be the one to discover that the things you really long for in your life are behind all the things you're holding so tightly to. You must be the one who finds clarity about the things you want in your life and the reason you're here on this earth.

What is your purpose?

What do you want out of your life?

Only you can answer those questions.

Let me show you how different my life is today than it was even a

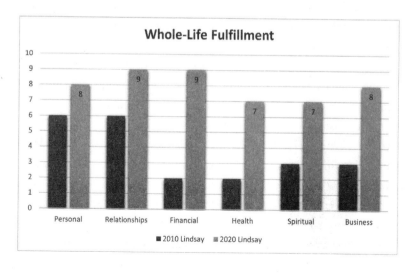

decade ago as I began to work toward the life I was thrilled to wake up to every day. Perhaps this will help you gain some insight into how this may play out in your own life as you start to make changes to the way you live and go about the business of building fulfillment, one area at a time rather than all at once.

The dark color is the level of fulfillment in my life in 2010, and the light represents my life in 2020, a decade later. In 2010, I was not thinking about my health or spiritual life very much at all (read: avoided it completely) because I felt like my time, effort, and resources were being gobbled up by my relationships, my kids, education, and the work I was doing at that time. I would have told you I didn't have the brain or life space to focus elsewhere when I had so many other obligations at that time. And that would have been the truth. Here's why.

In 2010 I was thirty years old. I had one-year-old twins and a brand-spanking-new little baby. Even with zero focus on health and spirituality, my life was chaos on most days. I was a year into my master's program. I worked a full-time corporate job from home that I absolutely hated and that used approximately none of my skills, talents, and gifts. My husband worked full-time outside of the house. My marriage was on young family cruise control, which involves a kiss in the morning and falling asleep on our faces at 7:45 p.m. each night. I lived in a new city in Colorado where I knew approximately one person. We were struggling financially, living in a rented house. I was trying to make my own baby food (because chemicals) and find ways to make extra income at the same time to afford such luxuries. My mother had suddenly and unexpectedly died of a massive, stress-induced heart attack. I wound up with the baby blues, eating my feelings every day and finding "happiness" in whatever thrill I could put on the calendar to look forward to. I was a subpar friend, I had a shitload of unmet potential, and to top it off, I was really frickin' mean to myself on most days.

We simply assume we always have more time to find fulfillment and happiness. Sing it with me now: "I'll staaaart Monday!" Make no mistake; avoidance isn't patience, avoidance isn't self-care, and avoidance isn't a virtue. The truth is that avoidance is a game I've played and lost so many times in my life and that has not once served me. If you want whole-life fulfillment, you have to wake up and tell avoidance it's no longer your bedmate.

Your turn. Begin charting your whole-life fulfillment progress. On a scale of 1–10, rate your level of fulfillment now versus ten years ago and fill out the chart below so you have a visual of your progress (or not, which is also normal and okay). You'll want to revisit it as you continue on.

Here's some data to consider as you do the work.

Whole-Life Fulfillment

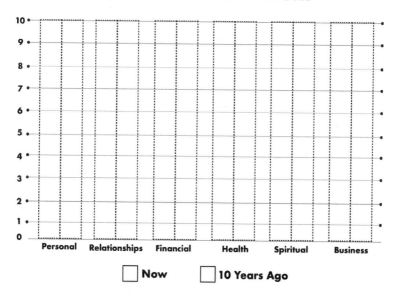

The average desired age of retirement is around sixty-six years old.[3] According to a recent study, a staggering 64 percent of Americans are now expected to retire with less than $10,000 saved.[4] The cost of a comfortable retirement is between $53,000 (Mississippi) and $125,000 (Hawaii) per year for the typical American, which varies based on the part of the country you live in.[5] Let's call that what it really is—broke. The math doesn't work. It doesn't take a genius to determine that less than $10,000 isn't going to last a year if it costs $53,000 to live.

Ten thousand dollars saved to live on for the rest of your life isn't "getting by," that's failure to thrive. Think of the savings amount as a symptom of a bigger problem. This increasingly common situation has a lot less to do with not making enough money and a whole lot more to do with having a mindset rooted in scarcity and fear. I recently read an article by Kevin Nast that listed the ten reasons most people don't prepare for retirement, and the answers were shocking.[6]

10. "I'm too busy."
9. "It's too soon."
8. "It's too late."
7. "I don't need to."
6. "I don't have enough money to get started."
5. "My finances are a mess."
4. "The government will take care of me."
3. "Between my savings and my 401(k), I'll be fine."
2. "I don't want to think about it."
1. "I don't know."

These answers aren't answers that lead me to believe that we as members of society are trying our best to prepare and are just missing the mark. "I don't know" was the number one answer. How easy is it to find information right now? You've heard of the World Wide Web, right?

No, these are answers of fear, avoidance, and lack of desire to dedicate resources to the cause. I think it has a lot to do with a lack of direction or understanding of our purpose. If we understood our purpose, wouldn't we be doing everything we could to continue it? I think it has a lot to do with what we've been conditioned to believe about money and about what makes us happy. You've likely heard the aphorism "Money is the root of all evil," but you'd be surprised how many people believe that and act accordingly, even unconsciously. I think it has a lot to do with fear, disappointment, failure, and what others think. I think it has a lot to do with ignoring reality and settling for "good enough" because we have too much other stuff taking up the time in our lives. We settle for believing we either do it all at the same time or we can't do it at all.

When I made the unconscious choice to focus on my personal life and building relationships (I had a young family at that time), I chose also to ignore certain parts of my life, resulting in lower-than-desired fulfillment in those areas. I thought all the time about my finances but didn't have the discipline or understanding to change that situation. My days were filled with little kids, snacks on snacks on snacks, making sure my husband was happy, cleaning, cooking, my hobbies, scheduling (and attending) kids' activities, and looking forward to that glass of wine with dinner. I also found myself doing a job I absolutely hated in order to pay the bills, and I had no plan to be fulfilled in that area. I laid fulfillment down in those areas and settled for contentment.

Here's a snapshot of where I was putting my time, energy, and resources in 2010:

2010 LINDSAY

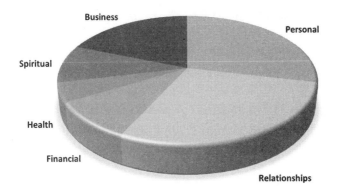

As I was ignoring problems in a few areas of my life (namely financial, business, spiritual, and health), they didn't just go away. Instead, I just settled for that constant, nagging feeling that true happiness and fulfillment were somewhere else, out of reach for me at the time. I could be happy in other ways. I was convinced that whole-life fulfillment was for others. I was convinced that giving up my own fulfillment was what good mothers do. More word manipulation, and I ate it all up because that excuse plays, doesn't it? Who's going to call someone out for playing small in their life and with their purpose when they're doing it for their kids? But let's be honest, is that the real reason? Nah. Are we really giving it up for the betterment of our kids? Nope. Do we believe a mom focused on her fulfillment is less capable than one who is ignoring her own needs? I certainly don't. Great parents know they can't pour from an empty cup. So, our excuse sucks.

Since the time I was a young girl, becoming a self-made millionaire as an entrepreneur was on my to-do list. I watched my parents struggle financially my entire life. Even up to the date of my mother's death, she struggled. I knew from a young age it would be up to me to break that cycle of scarcity and financial struggle and the pain of regret. One day I changed my mind about what I was allowed to do and what was best for not only me but those around me as well. In 2013, I decided to focus on finding fulfillment both financially and at work. I quit a job I hated and found myself with the choice to settle for being content or to push for something more. And I decided to push myself with everything in me. I was so tired of my bullshit excuses that it didn't even feel like a choice. It felt like the only option.

Here's the really interesting thing, though: because I was actively working on fulfillment in my relationships and my personal life, my baseline contentment levels were higher. Meaning, I expected my relationships and personal life to satisfy me and make me feel good. Any dip in those areas I would notice and feel a lot. But those areas didn't dip dramatically because the habits I had put in place to work on the relationships with my kids and husband were automatic. They actually gave me more drive to focus on success in those other areas knowing I could use the rewards for success to enhance my personal and relational fulfillment. I was able to translate my need for personal fulfillment and get those needs met through work and through financial gain. In fact, I now realize how much I leaned on my family and personal desires during that time as I dug into my business and finances. If I hadn't built a strong foundation in those areas, I don't believe financial or business success would have felt as sweet. This was the order of priority meant for me and the kind of life I wanted to build. Of course, there was struggle through the change in my marriage and the way I parented my kids, but my focus elsewhere didn't require me to give up on those two areas; they only enhanced my desire and need for change in my life.

It's interesting to note that a few good choices in these new areas led me to finding a much more consistent level of fulfillment in my whole life, not by focusing on everything at once, but by focusing on a few things with great clarity and energy. The confidence we gain when we get a win in our lives radiates into our next correct decision. By connecting my family and personal desires to financial and business success, I was able to give myself the kind of leverage needed to work at the pace and intense level of focus required for success. The result? This is what my life satisfaction looks like ten years later:

2020 LINDSAY

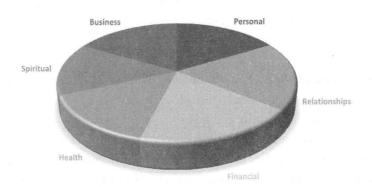

I believe that the actions I took around that time caused a ripple effect in my life that affected thousands of other people and gave me the confidence to believe I can do anything I set my mind to. I have an entire box of letters, cards, and notes from people who were affected by the way I was living my life because these kinds of ripples are hard to ignore. They're hard to tune out and gloss over because they radiate energy. They feel like a raging fire in a dark room, and those kinds of things demand the attention of others. Some people will see your changes and they'll be drawn to you like a magnet. Others will try their hardest to put your fire out because the way you live your life makes them feel some kind of way about themselves, and they're still in that numbing stage when things get hard. Remember that kind of energy isn't about you—that's about them.

We can create change in the lives of others simply by living ours like we give a shit about it—what a gift for your people. A gift that's not just words and postures but is revealed in action and feeling. That's what I want to do with my time on earth.

I want to live so loud and on fire that the people around me can't ignore it.

I want to live so authentically and joyfully that my kids will never settle for less because they know what's possible.

I want to live so fearlessly that it scares others to see what they're missing.

> I want to live so fearlessly that it scares others to see what they're missing.

I want my life to be a beacon of hope about what can be achieved if you decide to live on purpose.

You can live this way through the process of deconstructing the parts of your life that mean something to you and building them back in a way and in the order that feels the most correct for you. This process is about leaning into your purpose and your mission. It's about fulfilling your dreams. By doing so, you will affect others in a profound and tangible way. You'll inspire them, help them, show them, and lead them in a way you've never been able to do before simply by not settling for good enough. The simple process of becoming a fulfilled person will change everything around you.

A beautiful world is waiting for us; we just have to give ourselves the chance to believe it. We have to go back and discover who we are and what we want beyond our conditioning and traumas. We have to release the false sense of safety we're holding so tightly to in order to fly.

The simple process of becoming a fulfilled person will change everything around you.

And fly you will.

On wings so strong and certain that nothing, and I mean nothing, can keep you on the ground. You're meant to fly. I'm here to push you out of the nest. Even when you're scared, even when you think you can't, even when you think you shouldn't, I'm going to push you. Here's where I'm tempted to type, "I'm going to be the wind beneath your wings," but seriously. I'm going to do that because that's the only way a book can make you better. I can't "nice" you into change, but I can lead you to living on purpose.

PURPOSE AND FULFILLMENT

I believe we're all called and all given a purpose on earth. I don't believe we all accidentally wound up here together and we float through life on a giant rock in space to no end. No, I believe in your purpose. I believe my purpose is to be here to help you think differently about that purpose. I'm here to help you think in a way that moves you strategically closer to that purpose. I have a deep desire to live, work, and play around people who are working in their purpose. I love the way it feels. That energy, as we discussed earlier, is magnetic.

When we all live and walk in our purpose, we have the ability to feel true fulfillment. Not that kind of fulfillment that never produces a bad day. I'm talking about the kind of fulfillment that produces countless bad days but you feel the joy of living anyway. Your gratitude cannot be diminished. You get to see those bad days as a means to more good ones. You will eventually believe it and welcome every challenge with gusto and excitement for what lies behind it. But it won't happen overnight, and it won't happen if you have a closed mind about it. You have to believe it first, and then a whole world opens up to you.

What if you started to believe that you're already equipped to start using your gifts? What if your spirit told your mind who you really are? What if you stopped believing you have to become anything to achieve your purpose? Let me tell you something I believe down deep: you don't need to become anything to carry out your purpose. You're already that person. You've always been. It's time to discover and love yourself just as you are right now. It's time to set your true self free. It's time to tell yourself all the things you want to be true. It's time to tell yourself with certainty that you are her. It's time to create your future so that you can actually live it and not just wish for it.

Let's talk about what it means to live a life fulfilled.

You don't have to want anything more for your life. You don't. With a few exceptions around understanding his automated behavior responses and his bucket list items, my husband doesn't. He has, for his whole life, wanted to have a close relationship with his wife and kids, buy a house in cash, and make a million dollars in his thirties, which he has accomplished.

At this moment, he feels fulfillment in his six cornerstones. He doesn't need to accomplish anything more. He doesn't need to impress anyone like he did when he was striving at work. He doesn't need to prove his worth to others so he will be liked. He's got what he always wanted, and he's very happy and fulfilled with his life. He wants to experience his life, but he doesn't need more things. I'm amazed he had (and has) the ability to see what he wanted and has determined it is enough for him where he's at. You have to admit that's a baller move. He doesn't need something else to help him find fulfillment. Fulfillment is just a part of his everyday life as he interacts with the people he loves and builds a life that helps him meet his highest values each day.

Everyone gets to decide their level of fulfillment.

You can feel immense joy in your life right now—I do—and still know there's more out there for you to experience, or more ways you can expand your threshold of success in all areas. I believe life is about experiencing and learning new things every day so that we can teach those lessons to the people who are put in our path. Your goals or desires don't have to be about things. They can be about experiences, feelings you've shared, accomplishments, purpose, spiritual clarity, or new skills.

> Your goals or desires don't have to be about things. They can be about experiences, feelings you've shared, accomplishments, purpose, spiritual clarity, or new skills.

Success, significance, happiness, or fulfillment are stand-in words for personal power. What would it feel like to have personal power in every part of your life? Something's going horribly wrong in your business? You have the personal power to get into that office and pivot like a champ, and you can realize that this experience, this test, is making you stronger and more powerful in this area. Someone in your family is sick? You have the personal power to hit your knees and have a conversation with God about it. You have the personal power to rally what's needed to take care of your family member. You can do that because you've prepared your mind. And your power over any situation you find yourself in creates happiness despite tragedy because you know it's all for you.

You are worthy of fulfillment and "the good life," as my mom called it, but it doesn't come without a change, without a fight. Are you willing to step into the ring?

ENTITLEMENT MINDSETS ARE AN INFECTION OF THE MIND

THE TIMELINE OF CHANGE

Change is an elusive thing. It can feel hard. It, admittedly, takes a lot of work. It never looks like we think it will. And change is something that 90 percent of people have a problem with. In fact, 80 percent of people will refuse to change even given information about how it could prolong their life.[1] Change is often uncomfortable, and as a society, we are becoming more and more allergic to it.

MY TIMELINE

Change is something I wanted in my life for decades, and yet it seemed to elude me. I'd try to be different, and it never seemed to stick. There always seemed to be a missing piece to making permanent changes that were good for me. I think that's normal. Most of us would say the same was true in our own lives. We struggle to control our urges, desires, needs, and behaviors because we don't understand how to make lasting change.

In my early childhood, I experienced a lot of chaos. My parents struggled in almost every way—financially, relationally, spiritually, and personally, creating a lot of unrest within our family. At one point, we lived on the road, traveling the country in a brown-on-brown Chevy van. Are you getting Matt Foley vibes right now? Yes, we basically lived in a "van down by the river" at one point. I can remember sleeping in strangers' houses as we traveled from one city to the next while my dad performed at different churches and schools around the country. He was a singer/songwriter, and my two brothers, my mother, and I traveled around the United States as he performed in the evenings, and I homeschooled during the day. Weirdest backstory ever, I know, right? That time in my life felt really uncomfortable and out-of-the-ordinary. Probably because it was uncomfortable and out of the ordinary.

When I was entering second grade, our family ended up in Arizona for the next two decades of my life. My dad became a pastor, and my mom became the music leader for the church, which they started in our home on Sunday mornings. I learned a lot about how to build a business from the ground up at that time, so it wasn't all bad, but behind the scenes this was the part of my story where chaos began to turn into anger. My brothers and I started getting older and seeing things differently than we did as little kids. We had more information about how the world works, and we realized something was off at home.

Small cracks in the foundation of our family became gaping holes that couldn't be covered up with a few smooth words, control, threats, or a new distraction, as was typical in our family. Problems like addiction, violence, betrayal, and manipulation inside the walls of a pastor's home were not something we talked about. So, we pretended a lot. I was used to hearing the "This stays in our family" talk. It's similar to "What happens in Vegas stays in Vegas," but with a religious twist. When I hit around age twelve, I remember feeling so much confusion and anger about who I was, and I remember hating to be at home because it didn't feel like a safe space to be myself. It just wasn't a happy place for me. I felt like I always had to pretend, and I felt like a bad kid because I hid a lot from my parents, I lied, I wore a lot of masks to keep from being seen, and I kept a lot of secrets.

Eventually, I just stopped taking the masks off. I would morph into a different version of myself as I was conditioned to do and become who others wanted me to be. It was like being a chameleon of sorts. Not because someone told me to but because I thought this was the way to belong somewhere and everything at home would remain "status quo."

I was who my mom wanted me to be with her, which created resentment for many years. I was who my dad wanted me to be with him, which created anger and, at times, all-out rage. I was who would get the most attention with friends, which produced loneliness and disconnection. I was constantly putting on different masks to see which one would return love. Spoiler alert: none of them feel like love when you're faking it. Eventually, the deception became so easy for me that I became the version of me people expected without realizing I was pretending. I so easily would morph into who I perceived other people wanted me to show up as. I hadn't learned my lesson yet.

Before I go on, I want to state very clearly that my parents were flawed individuals, just like all of us, who were doing the best they could to get their own highest needs met. At the time it was really hard, but I'm so grateful for my story now. Through my upbringing I've been given a great advantage in my life. Through the struggle I learned more than I ever could have if I had grown up getting my every need met under Ward and June Cleaver's roof. Because of my past, I know very clearly what I want and do not want for my own family. I own every second of my story with great pride, even the parts where I was the bad guy—and I've been an asshole a lot in my life.

In my twenties I began trying to fill all of the holes left in my soul from betraying my true self over and over again. All I knew was something wasn't working because I wasn't "happy," and I began searching for the things that would help me numb the pain. I filled my life with a decade-long relationship with the wrong person, choosing to ignore every sign that it wasn't right. I used that relationship to fill the empty parts of me, and that wasn't fair to him. I filled my life with more education just so I would have something to do that made me feel like I mattered. I ate shitty food that destroyed my body, mind, and health, and I abused food for control. I made close friends with distractions like entertainment and adventure to numb myself. I made terrible money decisions and found myself in debt. The worst part of all was that I hid most of my actions from others so they'd never know the real me. I filled those holes as fast as I could because they're uncomfortable to look at and damn near unbearable to feel.

It's my bet that it wouldn't take long for you to identify a few moments like this in your own life. I can feel the collective nervousness as you start connecting my story to yours, especially where it intersects over behavior we aren't proud of. And the following question is usually, "Okay, Lindsay, that's great for you, but how do I do it?"

I promised to help you find your way to the good life, not that it would always feel good. Shame is off-limits, though, so if you're reading this and shaming yourself, you need to get control of your mindset because shame will keep you stuck until death if you let it.

In my thirties, I was determined to find bliss because I had watched my mother pass away and realized very quickly that my days to find fulfillment were limited. I could, just like my mom, be here one day and gone the next. It is not lost on me that the last thing she talked to me about before she died were the things she wished she had done when she was my age. For an hour and a half she sat on the phone with me and changed my life, though I didn't understand that at the time. She had no idea her time was up, and I thought she'd never die. It was a true shock in my life when my husband sat me down to tell me the horrifying news.

I took very little time (like two weeks) to grieve before I threw myself into my life (work, side hustle, raising my three tiny babies, and my master's program) because that was my standard operating procedure. I let my regret for my mom fuel me to figure this puzzle out. I suddenly made a mental shift to say, "No more." I absolutely did not want to think about leaving this world and my kids without having done the things that make life worth living. I didn't want them to feel for me like I feel for my mom. I kept searching for fulfillment, but this time I was really tired of my own BS. I'd tried to numb everything, and it never worked. I was going to try something new.

I began breaking down the things I wanted into the feelings I wanted to feel. I didn't want things; I wanted feelings. Rather than seeing a trip as something really fun for me or something to check off the list, I thought about the feelings that I would feel during that adventure, and I began to let that motivate me. Instead of making a goal to make a million dollars, I started chasing the feelings that success would bring me and what it would feel like to watch others do the same.

Those feelings started finding me everywhere I went, as long as I was willing to do the hard work of identifying them and making them feel real in my mind.

Instead of wanting to build a successful business so I could be seen, I started working to create a place for others to belong.

I started figuring out who I was at my core and identifying the things that I value. I started to hear my inner voice. I started to set boundaries. I began working toward goals that matched my personal values and not my traumas and secret shames. Instead of wanting to build a successful business so I could be seen, I started working to create a place for others to belong. Within three years of my mom's death, I made my first million dollars as an entrepreneur.

- I started meditating and praying on the things that would get me closer to my purpose.
- I started thinking about the things that were missing in my life and decided to show up authentically to meet those needs.
- I started chasing positive and high-vibrational feelings and emotions.
- I started taking off the mask and letting the feelings that greet me when others don't like me pass right through me.

- I took control of the way I spoke to myself and others.

All one small step at a time until I was no longer that twelve-year-old in a mask.

In the past decade, I just kept pushing for more because more was out there for me. Each time I'd accomplish something I wanted, I'd let that momentum carry me to the next mountain to climb. What else is out there in this great big world just waiting for the authentic version of myself to show up? And the things that were for me, found me. The things that weren't, didn't. I learned how to not push doors open for myself. I learned to be patient. I learned to implement better habits in my life.

Man, my thirties were so hard and so life-giving at the same time. Even with all of the hard, I was raising a family I loved, I had built some great businesses that paid me enough to never have to work again, I bought my house in cash, I traveled the world, I spoke to thousands of women, I wrote books, and I ate at restaurants I dreamed about. I had built a lot of fulfillment in four of the six cornerstones of a good life, but my health and spiritual life were on life support.

Who lives the kind of life I was living and has the massive lady balls to ask for more? Just who did I think I was to want more on top of that "success" that others saw? The question constantly swirled in my mind, *You think you deserve more? There are people out there who don't have a fraction of what you have in your life. Why more? Why now? Isn't that selfish?* I'd think of the mistakes I'd made, the people I had hurt, the failures I couldn't erase from my history, the terrible choices I had made, and my rational mind said no. But my spirit said something different. My spirit whispered quietly, *None of that matters; there's more for you here. You're uniquely qualified for your dreams—all of them.*

As I reflect on these feelings of deservedness that I still battle from time to time, I realize that I don't deserve anything. None of us do. I'm not entitled to a nice life just because someone else has one; I have to earn it. In the same way, I am not disqualified from more just because others may believe it enough. I don't deserve a great family; I am charged with the duty to build one if I want it. I don't deserve to live to ninety-eight; I have to work for it, even if others don't. Entitlement mindsets are an infection of the mind. Little by little, it will destroy your ability to do the extraordinary.

Eventually, I found myself asking the correct question: *Is what's left for me worth giving up what I have? What if my family doesn't understand? What if my husband is tired of me constantly getting into something new? What will this do to my friendships if I change my mind about what I believe? Will I be able to love my life if I focus on making my health a priority?* To which the only answer is and always will be, *Wait and see.*

I found the answer to be yes. Yes, working on my health changed a lot of my personal goals. I had to let go of some of what previously made me feel fulfilled—things like my daily pick-me-up sweet tea and calling a hot bath, a book, and a tub of Cinnamon Bears "self-care." Seeking a new relationship with God did change some of my friendships and my relationship with my husband. Each new thing I lean into changes me, and I'm no longer trying to control that. I'm just letting what happens happen. I'm being present and noticing changes. I'm allowing the new to find me, and I'm not hanging onto the old. These simple acts of letting go have created so much ease in my life. It feels like I was squeezing the blade of a knife for so long and I finally realized I can just open my hand and let the wound heal.

Fear of the unknown is a real thing. Fear is what stops most of us from taking the kind of action that change requires. As soon as we begin associating change with words like *loss* or *despair*, we recoil. We want the good without the bad. The problem is that we've labeled the emotions we aren't comfortable with as "bad." We need to change that. Those uncomfortable feelings are not bad. In fact, embracing them head-on is exactly what we need to do to get to the good life.

> Fear is what stops most of us from taking the kind of action that change requires.

So I want to talk about the behaviors that keep us from creating the change we want in life. I want to call them out, up front so you're aware of them and you can identify them as soon as you see them creep into your inner dialogue or mindset. And I want to arm you with tools to help you better understand and navigate your path to whole-life fulfillment.

TIME TRUTHS

One thing we know will bring change (or not) is time. Perhaps one of the biggest holdbacks for you to make lasting change is that you've believed the myth that there just isn't enough time. You don't have enough time in your day, in your year, or in your life to find fulfillment.

Hold up, I'm about to shove a stick of dynamite into that excuse.

I recently started following an amazing woman on social media named Joan MacDonald because her story captured my heart. Joan is a seventy-five-year-old, silver-haired beauty. Her smile radiates joy and thirst for more life. You can feel her energy through the screen. The reason I started following Joan is because she started exercising and working on her nutrition at the age of seventy and at almost two hundred pounds. Her transformation is incredible for any age, but seventy? You should see her guns. Joan doesn't play. She's lost over sixty-five pounds so far and said that the work to get there was "totally worth it."[2] She changed her physical body and health at the age of seventy. We've all got the time.

Where are you in your life right now? How many dreams did you have when you were younger that you have moved on from or you've run out of time for? Don't worry, this thought doesn't have to be depressing. I've recognized that many of my dreams aren't even my own. They're what I *think* I want, for reasons I have been taught to believe. Maybe you always wanted to earn a certain degree, succeed in corporate America, have a certain number of kids, or have a specific dollar amount in the bank. Maybe you're on your way to achieving the dream. Maybe you're not. Whatever the case, take some time to truly ask yourself:

- What are your dreams?
- Are your dreams for you, or are they to change how others perceive you?
- How many of your dreams are for other people?
- Why are we working for the approval of another human being?
- What gives those people the power to be in charge of how much you do and how you do it?
- How did someone else's opinion become part of your life plan?

Answering these questions is likely to uncover some blind spots you didn't even know were showing up in your decision-making process. Once these blind spots are gone, you can freely focus your time on the changes you'll make for you.

Here's the way I think about change connected to time. When I think about the plans I have for my life, I think about them in terms of years I have to pull them off. I want you to do the same in the next activity. This isn't one of those activities that is meant to bum you out. This activity is meant to make you face reality and see it for what it really is. If your goal is to run a marathon because you know it's going to help you get in shape, prove you have a strong mindset, and perhaps help clear your mind, great. Realistically, how many years do you have left to make training a priority and meet your goal?

I base my "time to get this completed" for work, finances, family relationships, and health on the age of fifty. Fifty is when my kids will be out of the house and on their own (presumably). Fifty is the year I hope to retire from day-to-day work. Fifty is the age where I believe I'll have gained a decent amount of wisdom and my body will still cooperate with me. I actually want no plans for what to do or who to become after fifty. I've changed so much in the first four decades of my life, why wouldn't that still be the case? I want to be free to travel, take dance lessons, watch the sunset, learn how to paint, or become a certified yogi if that's what my heart desires. I want nothing on the calendar after fifty other than freedom.

That means I really only have ten years to make sure I've built personal power in each of the six areas of my life. Ten years left to make sure my finances are in order so I can live on the interest of my investments or passive income. I have ten more years to figure out the way I want to spend my time after retirement and earmark the right amount of funds for that. I have ten years to build a relationship with my husband that will flourish for the rest of our lives. I have ten years to show my kids how much they mean to me and nurture the kind of relationship I want with them before they're adults raising their own families. I have ten years to get my health in order before my bad choices become major obstacles to living an active life (or living a life at all, to be honest). I evaluate everything I take on through the lens of the amount of time I have to pull it off, and if it doesn't fit, I'm out. Simple as that.

I want you to fill in the graph on the next page with the weeks of your life you've already lived. For each week you've been alive, fill the box in completely. If you don't have an age in mind, that's okay. The average life expectancy in 2020 was 78.9 years.[3] Let's just round that up to eighty for ease of understanding and because we always defy the odds, *nomsayin*? This is going to give you a visual of the amount of life you've already lived and the amount of time you have left.

A little scary to look at those blanks and realize that's all the time you may have left to figure this whole fulfillment thing out. I look back on the years I've already lived and realize how much time I spent doing things that would please others or bring me a temporary feeling. Some days it feels like a waste, but it never was. That time was spent trying things and learning. There's nothing wasted about that. The only reason I'm here writing this and helping you uncover what will set your soul on fire is because of those years spent chasing the wrong thing. How can you know what's right for you if you never know what's wrong for you?

Now, here's the thing about time. We tend to believe we can get more done in the short-term than we really can. And we tend to underestimate how much we can achieve in the long-term. That means we take on too much in a short amount of time and don't take on enough in a long

amount of time. That has to stop if you want to live in reality and not in a fantasy world.

If you're starting to get sweaty and think, *I'm too old for this*, we need to talk. As long as you can learn, you have the ability to create and share. You have the ability to create fulfillment in your life no matter how much time you have left (remember Joan). You can create change in your life instantly, right now, just by following the steps laid out in this book. I'm not saying you have time left in your life to cross off everything on your bucket list. I'm saying you have enough time to see and find fulfillment before your time is up.

Awareness is the first step, and you have that. You're now aware of how much time you have left before your eightieth birthday. If you were to believe that each of those weeks could help you discover the things that will bring you true fulfillment, what would hold you back? What do you have to lose besides everything that keeps you from that state of self-actualization, even if it feels like hard work?

PUTTING IT IN ORDER

Now we know how much time we have left until we're eighty. That kind of exercise puts your time into perspective, doesn't it? The next step is to figure out what order you want to tackle this in. As I said, balance isn't something you can achieve by trying. I don't think you can do all things in all six areas of your life and have time to feel fulfillment; the short-term to-do list becomes too long and the pressure to perform too great. Personally, I've never seen anyone be able to build a life that feels totally put together and fulfilled while pushing really hard in one certain area of life. It's going to ebb and flow as you put your energy into different parts of your life. You can give yourself permission to go in any order at any pace that is correct for you.

The people I know who try to do it all end up burned out and unhappy with the number of things on their plate. It's going to be really difficult to land the job you want or build the business that brings in the millions of dollars you desire so that you can go to all the places and do all the things. Especially if you have a spouse, kids, extended family, and friends to care about all while you work out every day and eat whole, organic foods to support your body. Also, don't forget about connecting with God every day and spending time in prayer and meditation with Him. You will get to the place where you've created amazing habits and structure around your day to work through your list of priorities, and you will operate at a higher level, but don't expect the changes to happen all at once.

You won't have much time to rest or enjoy the things that make you smile if you're shoving too much growth into your day. Your life isn't meant to be all work, but it is meant to be mostly learning. The minute you quit learning and taking in new information to better your life is the minute you become old. And I don't mean old in age, I mean old in spirit.

> Your life isn't meant to be all work, but it is meant to be mostly learning.

That's the time you throw your hands up and say, "There is nothing more I can do here." Be realistic about the effort it takes to create a habit, and give yourself space to screw it all up sometimes. When I'm learning something new, other things in my life become affected quite often. Don't build your house on a poorly built and half-assed foundation. This stuff takes mind work, concentrated effort, and time. Build slow, build strong, and before you build, let's get your mind in check.

CHANGING YOUR MIND

Do you realize that "95% of who we are by the time we're 35 years old is a memorized set of behaviors, emotional reactions, unconscious habits, hardwired attitudes, beliefs, and perceptions that function like a computer program"?[4] You know why? Because your mind and body are machines. Because this is what your machine does to make living life as safe as possible so that you can live as long as possible. Imagine that.

Ninety-five percent of what you do is automated without you being conscious to it.[5] So that means that 95 percent of your potential is waiting for you through consciousness and awareness. You've got 95 percent more juice in the tank. Just by thinking about your thoughts and becoming an observer in your life you have a huge advantage on the road to whole-life fulfillment over the people you know or interact with who live their lives asleep. The process of figuring yourself out and identifying the voice inside your head will point you in new directions, toward new ideas and new possibilities.

Stop getting out of bed the same way, interrupt your patterns, try a new route, see new people, put your pants on two legs at a time, get out of the program your mind has created for you to live in.

When we make decisions in a state that is programmed into us, it happens subconsciously, and our mind doesn't pay as close attention. Your mind wants you to remain safe and asleep; this is a hindrance to a new mental shift. So remember that you get to control what you let into your mind; you get to decide what's true about things your mind tells you, not the other way around. You can say things like I did—"I want to be healthy, I want to feel freedom, I want to be happy"—but if your body is on a program that says the opposite, there will be no lasting change. You have to interrupt the program and then say what you want and why you want it and then give yourself enough leverage to force a change in your programming. Creating leverage in your life is like backing yourself into a corner. You have no choice but to take action. You will create new programming that pushes your mind past your previous threshold of success. You have to get into your subconscious mind and blow that bitch up.

You don't need to wait for a crisis. You don't need to wait for your body to fail you. You don't need to wait for someone to give you permission. You don't need to wait until you feel differently. Your programming isn't going to allow that kind of significant change without you telling it to.

I have a friend who often feels like she doesn't give much value to others because she doesn't have a lot of big trauma in her past. Her mind says to her, *What can you teach others when you haven't had the hardship that they have? How can you help if you haven't had to overcome major traumas in your life?* That story she's telling herself is so limiting but I understand it because that's how we're programmed.

We often believe that change comes through only hardship and tragedy, but it doesn't have to. Your life story can be healthy and beautiful, and from that, amazing things can happen. Additionally, the things we believe are hardship and tragedy don't have to be that if we choose not to see them that way. Your perception of your life's events matters. There isn't one hard day that I wish away, not even the ones where I was the "victim." There isn't one day I'd do over. There isn't one crappy message from someone who doesn't know me that I'd wish away, even the ones that are downright nasty. Instead of being crushed under the opinions of others, I've learned to rise beyond the opinions of others. Instead of falling into the same emotional eating pattern when something blows up my day, I've learned to identify the part of me that needs some TLC and some truth.

I'm committed to introducing you to the possibility of what your life can be and to giving you as much help as possible as you discover it. You can learn to change in hardship or in joy if you learn to tune into your mind and disrupt the patterns you've fallen victim to without your consent.

> We often believe that change comes through only hardship and tragedy, but it doesn't have to.

I was introduced to this idea in my twenties and I'm still learning about it. I believe I'll be learning about this until the day that I die. I've discovered that this is the only way I want to live, in the process of continual growth, and sharing it with you adds value to my life.

IF I'M NOT CHANGING MY MIND I'M NOT LEARNING

THE FOUR ENDOWMENTS AND
THE TWELVE UNIVERSAL LAWS

Think about a time you might have flipped out about something small and not understood why.

Are you constantly worried about how you're going to be perceived by others? Have a constant need to numb yourself in front of a TV? Those are most likely actions from your trauma brain. Let me explain that.

Imagine your mind has an office manager named Peg. Peg sounds like a good office manager name. She's probably very organized and works efficiently after a couple cups of coffee, and she probably brings donuts into the office a few times a month for the crew. Peg's pretty cool. When you experience normal days, Peg will take all of the things you experienced, like what you felt, tasted, heard, smelled, and saw, and file it away in the proper places in your mind in separate folders. Let's pretend that when you were a kid you used to cut the grass at your grandpa's house when you'd go to visit. The smell of the grass and gasoline, the sound of the mower, how the grass looked, and how it felt when the mower would shake your hands would all be filed away in your mind in the proper folders.

Now you're thirty years old and you're out mowing your own yard for the first time. You take in the first whiff of fresh-cut grass and gasoline. Your office manager goes to the filing cabinet in your olfactory system and pulls out the *Fresh-Cut Grass and Gasoline* file. She opens it up and you remember a time at your grandpa's house. That smell brought you right back to that day. You smile and move along with your day. Well done, Peg, another successful day at the office. You're able to process that memory and move along with your day.

Peg is really efficient at filing your good times away properly, but she's not as on the ball when things turn south. Now let's imagine that you encounter and experience some trauma in your life. You were driving one rainy day and out of nowhere, another driver T-boned your car going through the intersection. You suffered some injuries, and you thought your heartbeat would never return to normal, but you survived. Your mind will be going crazy trying to protect you from danger and death, and you'll have a lot to file away. Peg's to-do list is about to get nuts. The sensory input is moving so fast that sometimes, Peg will take everything you just experienced and instead of filing them in their proper place, she'll just put everything in one big red file. She isn't sure what to do with this huge file, and she's not really looking for much overtime these days, so she closes the file and puts it in the closest drawer she can find and clocks out early for the day. There's just too much to do right now to file it separately.

One day a few years later you're in the passenger seat of a car and it's raining outside again. The light in front of the car turns yellow and your husband hits the gas to make it through the light (safely, mind you). Suddenly, Peg remembers she's seen this input before—rainy and driving—and she pulls out the big red folder and asks, *Remember this?* Only this time, instead of remembering just the sound or the feeling, you suddenly feel it all. The whole folder from that accident is opened, and you're scared out of your mind even though you're totally safe. You feel all of that fear and frustration all over again and turn to your husband and light his ass up. You may start shaking and feeling like you did on that day. But why? You're safe, remember?

Everything you've ever experienced is in your mind filed away, we just can't always retrieve it. Sometimes Peg files it right, and sometimes she needs some help. I found myself overreacting or avoiding things in my life that I didn't always understand, and in order to find fulfillment, I decided to seek some help for Peg.

In 2019 I went on a search for a behavioral counselor, someone who could help me identify the behaviors I often demonstrate that make absolutely no sense to me. I once got outrageously pissed off at my husband for pointing playfully at me and tapping his finger on my chest. He was clearly playing, but for some reason it made my blood turn hot, my body flushed, and I immediately went into fight mode. I'm talking full-on "cash me ousside, how 'bout dat" style. Something in the way it felt when his index finger tapped on my breastbone was an emotional trigger from my childhood. And in this case, I instantly knew what it was. My dad used to do that to me when he was really mad at me. All the feelings of rage that little Lindsay kept inside as a little girl bubbled up to the surface.

Again, let me be clear, he was doing his best, and my reaction to him is not his responsibility, it's mine. I don't want to hold on to the feelings; I want to work through them. I needed to help Peg file that event in the right folders so I didn't have to feel like that every time my husband or a friend is being playful with me. That was a trauma I hadn't processed, and it wasn't serving me all jumbled up in a single red folder any longer as it did when I was a child. This is why counselors and therapists are worth every red cent, especially if you are wanting to wake up to bigger and better change in your life. This kind of change sometimes requires additional help, and a counselor is trained to guide you through the hard shifts without judgment, shame, or agenda.

As I was unpacking some baggage with my counselor one afternoon, he told me about the four endowments and the twelve universal laws to help me put some of my decisions in perspective. He was using the laws to help me understand how the universe works and what my part really was in my traumas. What it did for me over the following year as I studied them was change a lot of the ways in which I see the world. I want to share them with you because they were so integral in my change process.

First, a little about both topics. There are four endowments every human possesses. An endowment is a gift given by God to everyone on the planet. You've likely heard this word used at the beginning of the United States Declaration of Independence. "We hold these truths to be self-evident: That all men are created equal; that they are *endowed* by their Creator with certain unalienable rights; that among these are life, liberty, and the pursuit of happiness." What a beautiful and life-giving string of words. Also, if you didn't read that first part like you're a Schuyler sister on a Broadway stage, I don't know what to tell you except, you did it wrong. An endowment is something bestowed upon us by our creator. Not by man or earthly means, but by something supernatural. You didn't know we were going to get so spiritual, did you? Buckle up. These endowments are your permission slip to go wild and live big in the way you've been called to—in the way that is stitched into the very fabric of your soul.

Additionally, there are twelve universal laws that I want to go through with you to give you some guidelines on mindset shifts you may need to make before understanding or pursuing big changes in your life. When I was presented this information in counseling two years ago, I changed my mind about a lot of things I was sure about just minutes before. I think you may find the same to be true. The twelve laws are universal, meaning that they are the same for you, me, and everything on this planet. These twelve laws govern the unchanging way our universe works.

THE FOUR ENDOWMENTS

If you've had the pleasure of reading Stephen Covey's writing, you've probably heard of the four human endowments.[1] I want to touch on them quickly because it's important to your growth to understand them. The four endowments are self-awareness, conscience, independent will, and creative imagination. God gave each of us these four gifts. This is the ultimate freedom. Let's quickly break the endowments down:

SELF-AWARENESS

You were given the gift of awareness, which allows us to step outside of our feelings and conscious mind and observe ourselves. Think of your body and mind as "me" and your spirit and observer as "I." As your awareness of your body and mind increases, your ability to flow with it and direct it also increases. Awareness creates more awareness in what feels like a landslide to me. It started slow, and now I am taking me for a ride. So often it works the other way around.

CONSCIENCE

This endowment, which helps you discern what is correct or incorrect for you, is sometimes depicted as the devil and the angel on your shoulder. This is your internal compass. My conscience often tells me when I'm having troubles with my boundaries because I have a tendency to ignore them to be liked. Our conscience keeps our actions in line with our principles and keeps us headed toward the things our spirit longs for.

INDEPENDENT WILL

This endowment basically gives us the ability to choose what we want, to respond how we want, and to change anything we want at any time in our lives. We have been given the gift of autonomy over our lives as free people. I love this one because I've found that most of my successes were built on the back of my mistakes. My independent will has taught me what I do and what I do not want, and I'm so grateful for this gift.

CREATIVE IMAGINATION

You were given the gift of creative imagination to cast visions about your life and what you want to achieve or experience. This endowment will lead you to finding solutions to problems or new iterations of an idea that might not have panned out. I like to think of creative imagination as the spoonful of sugar that helps the medicine go down. You'll know that there is more out there for you because you can see it in your mind's eye.

Like a muscle, you can strengthen your ability to use your endowments. The more you're aware of these endowments, the stronger your ability to choose the correct path. The more you use them, the more you hear them. Self-awareness, conscience, independent will, and creative imagination beget more of the same.

Choose healing. That's all you have to do. Consciously choose it, become aware of your thoughts and actions, interrupt your negative thought patterns, and then choose the change. Don't worry, I'm going to walk you through this in all six areas, and you can then create the change in the order that best suits your goals, needs, desires, calling, passions, and purpose. The fulfillment you are chasing is in that process. And it feels so right—not always good, but right, as in correct. Don't fool yourself into believing that all this change is going to feel like a summer evening. It might feel more like a thunderstorm. Better learn to dance in the rain.

THE TWELVE UNIVERSAL LAWS

There are twelve universal laws that are intrinsic and unchanging.[2] They've been around for centuries associated with culture, philosophy, and intuition. Honestly, they seemed a little "woo-woo" to me until they were explained to me in a way where I could see the proof in my own life. It was then I realized "universal" really means the entire universe is governed under these laws, and I'm not an exception just because I was naive to it or didn't see it in my life. Understanding these universal laws helps us navigate our story and focus our efforts in the right place. They also help us understand what changes are out of our control, an area where I have wasted hours, days, and years of my life.

THE UNIVERSAL LAW OF DIVINE ONENESS

This law basically states that we're all one. The same life energy that is in me is the same life energy that is in you. I love this one because it proves that we really are more alike than we are different. We are all humans who make mistakes on our path, and that common bond unites us. The energy that moves me through my life is the same energy that moves you through yours. The way we use them is up to us, individually.

Since yoga has become a part of my life in the last year, I've become more familiar with the word *namaste*, which means "I bow to you" or, put another way, "the sacred in me honors the sacred in you." When I become aware and make choices that are for my own fulfillment, I feel like I'm in a sacred space. I'm on the right path. That energy isn't unique to me. It's in all of us. I believe that source of sacred energy is from God and placed in each of us individually, uniting and bonding us together. Some people believe this energy is from the universe. Some believe in another deity altogether. I'm not here to tell you what or who created you or put you on this planet, I'm just here to open the door for you to explore that.

We are a part of the energy source so complicated and so vast that the human mind cannot comprehend it. Your thoughts, emotions, feelings, experiences, and actions are all affected by this energy through frequency. Often when I feel stressed out, I have a desire to be in nature. I want to walk in grass or touch the earth. I want to sit under trees and feel the earth's heartbeat. That's because I innately know I'm a part of that earth; we share energy.

The law of divine oneness has helped me so much with forgiveness, which was a struggle for me in early adulthood. That changed when I put into perspective that the same divine energy that lives in me and allows me to experience this life is the same in every other living person. We are connected in that way, and I believe we are meant to experience this life with others in community.

THE UNIVERSAL LAW OF VIBRATION

This is the law that changed my mind about all living things. This law states that everything around us is in constant motion and vibrates at a certain frequency, including us. Our body has a vibrational frequency, and everything we interact with can change that frequency. Follow me here.

We've all heard the phrase "good vibes only." It isn't just a pop-culture phrase millennials say to boomers who threaten to ruin their day, or a pithy saying for an overpriced T-shirt. It's bigger than that. Good vibrations physically vibrate at a higher frequency. So happy emotions or highly energetic vibrations will be changed by the vibrations of something or someone else that may not be vibrating as high. Negative emotions create low-frequency vibrations. Interacting with or connecting with someone with lower vibrational energy will rub off on you because, again, we are all connected through the universal law of divine oneness. Our vibrational energies inform or influence our lived experience.

Have you ever seen those videos online of what happens when you talk nicely to one plant and say hateful things to another? It's absolutely wild. The plants that receive your high vibrations grow and thrive while the plants that receive your low vibrations wilt and die. Your vibrational energy is strong. Strong enough to kill a plant, apparently! I talk to the plants in my backyard now if they're struggling to take root or grow. I have a real relationship with one of the vines on my back porch at this point.

If you've ever thought to yourself, *This place has a weird vibe* or *That person has a weird vibe*, that's your mind trying to make sense of the shift in vibrational energy between you and that place or that person. Anything and everything we come in contact with can influence our reality because we are fearfully and wonderfully made to sense that energy intuitively. Hey, that's the power of good vibes. I don't make the rules.

I remember when I was growing up, the idea of connecting energy was strictly off-limits in my ultraconservative, fear-based religious upbringing. Anything that resembled New-Age thinking was deemed witchcraft or off-limits. The more I study the world and the way God created us, the more I understand there is no fear in exchanging energy. There is no reason to deny its existence or pretend it's not of God because the one thing we know about God is that we don't know God. How can I imagine an all-powerful God who would equip us with emotions, complex feelings, and intuition but not one who could string all of that together in an energy we can feel? I can't.

The God I believe in is all-powerful, all-knowing, and in all places and things. Why wouldn't it feel like a vibrational energy? Why wouldn't it connect us to the earth and our people and everything we interact with? Why wouldn't we be able to evaluate what is meant to connect with us on this level? God is so much bigger than I ever let Him be in my mind. I'm just waking up to that.

The law of vibration tells us that if we want something in our life, we must align our energy in order to attract it. That makes sense to me. If I really want something, I have to be ready to receive it. How many stories have you heard about people who win or inherit a bunch of money and end up losing it all? How many people want something but as soon as they get it, they have a hard time hanging on to it? Their energy was operating at a lower vibrational level than needed to keep the money or that thing that they want so badly in their life. Higher energy attracts high energy, and vice versa.

The universal law of vibration goes back to holding your life and the things in it with an open hand. Anything meant for you at this time in your life is going to stay with you. Until you become the person ready to handle money, you'll never have it in the way you want it. Until you become the person who is capable of the goals you have in your life by operating at that energy level, it will never stay. When you feel irritated (which is a low-level energy in your body), remember to thank it for the lesson (Marie Kondo–style) and then let it go. You must live your life in the energy of what you want to attract. State what you want as a fact or as something you have already achieved. This is why affirmations work. Be what you want to be, and it will find you. Combine your thoughts and your feelings to create the kind of energy you want to attract into your life, and, like magic, it will find you.

THE UNIVERSAL LAW OF ACTION

This law states that in order for any of these laws to apply to you specifically, you must take action. The things you want will absolutely not appear out of the sky as if from nowhere. They will happen because you make them happen. If you don't get them, it won't be due to a lack of desire on your part but a lack of action aligned with your values and goals.

This is where we go back to the idea of flow. Doing something that you're passionate about and love to do should challenge the hell out of you but it should also be something that flows from you. When I watch my husband prepare for literally anything, I can see this flow in action. It challenges his mind to think of what we might need or what might come up that he needs to be prepared for, and it also comes easy to him.

> Don't make the mistake of driving your excitement into the ground doing activities or working on projects or skills that aren't really for you.

Ninety-nine percent of the time, Michael can reach into his bag and pull out the thing I forgot or whatever we might need at a given time. He is in flow when he's in prep mode. He shines when he starts to lay out problems that may arise. He has saved my butt hundreds of times simply because preparation for problems is one of his talents.

What Michael should not do in this case is set himself up to work hard on something that he has absolutely no interest in. We have preferences for a reason. They lead us to our bliss, gifts, talents, and joy. Writing is that for me, but it's far from that for Michael. Writing doesn't flow for him like it does for me. Remember to take your preferences into account when you start taking action. Don't make the mistake of driving your excitement into the ground doing activities or working on projects or skills that aren't really for you. Your excitement level is like fuel for action. Adjust, pivot, change your mind, try it a different way quickly before your mind convinces you to just give up trying—that quitter's mindset will come for you if you continuously try to shove a square peg into a round hole.

We're talking about the law of action. So, make your actions inspired by your spirit. Let yourself gravitate toward the activities that are exciting to you or inspire you to new heights, paths, and discoveries. This law requires a quiet mind at times, something I struggle mightily with. I'm not the one who typically hears that still, small voice, opting instead to hear only what makes a whole lot of noise. That usually comes in the form of pain, frustration, anger, resentment, and procrastination. Create space to hear your spirit tell you what to try. Sit in meditation more. Be quiet and observe around you. Look for signs. Be ready for new ideas. Invite those things into your life but sit quiet and be ready for the answers. Remember that the best time to take action is after you've rested, so don't just get quiet, get some good sleep.

Filling your life up with things to do is a great way to miss the lighted sign pointing to a new destination for you. If you're like me and struggle with shutting the hell up for like five seconds to breathe, don't be afraid to force yourself. I make meditation a priority in my day. I still lose the day and miss at times, but not very often. Let go of how you expect something to work and be open to the completely unexpected. Some of the least-expected outcomes have come from being open to giving things a try and letting my spirit lead me from there. The bottom line is if you're going to refuse to take any action, you might as well throw the rest of these laws out the window.

THE UNIVERSAL LAW OF CORRESPONDENCE

This one, it's not easy to swallow. This law states that what you see outside of you is a reflection of your insides. I saw this play out so many times during 2020, and I know you did too. The people who were unhappy before became extremely unhappy during the lockdown. It was simply more of the same inside feelings reflected outside for them. As I've stated before and I'll continue to say, you get to choose your mindset and how you view the things that "happen to you." Think of the Hermes quote, "As above, so below. As within, so without."[3] That sums up the law of correspondence.

This is one of my favorites of the twelve laws, and I find it to be one of the most life-changing. The idea of "This is happening for you, not to you" is rooted in this law. You can choose to see it either way, but I promise you, whatever it is you feel will reflect outward, and no, you won't be able to hide it.

My friend Joy is possibly the most outwardly happy and positive person I know. On the inside, though, she had some work to do, especially around her worth. At one point, the way she felt about her personal, spiritual, financial, work, and relational life started to spill outward, and I noticed the changes in her energy immediately. There were small changes in how she chose to show up in the world that felt like a smoke signal to the changes on the inside. It was clear there was something she was avoiding. And then one day she woke up and decided to put her own needs above those of the people who chose not to value her. She made the conscious decision to see her past traumas, mistakes, and failures that made her feel not enough as a gift to lead her to something better. I could actually feel it on her when I was around her following that choice.

Within a year, she got a divorce, walked away from her business, started traveling and hanging out with different people, changed her hair, started examining her religious beliefs, and went to work on a plan to make herself financially independent. She began making choices that supported her dreams for herself and not those of the people around her or her circumstances. Who she is today is that same person but with her hair on fire for her life. She's got more energy than any other person I know in their fifties. She radiates joy when her inside feels it. That joy simply comes from living in her purpose and prioritizing her own fulfillment—one step at a time. Each correct choice she felt on the inside radiated to the outside.

It's probably a good idea to get your journal out and list off the ways you're feeling about certain parts of your life. Notice how if you feel them on the inside they're likely showing on the outside. When my husband is in his head and gets caught up in his anxieties and fears, he has a tendency to snap at whoever the first person is to interrupt his train of thought. Within minutes, he'll be right there apologizing. And I've learned that that's just his inside showing on the outside. It's not about us; it's about him.

THE UNIVERSAL LAW OF CAUSE AND EFFECT

This is the cause-and-effect relationship that many people refer to as karma—the idea that what you do will come back to you. I think this one has a lot more to do with the consequences for your actions than a mystical force that rights all wrongs.

It's my belief that the consequences for your actions are for your gain (see the law of correspondence). So, no matter how much it hurts, it's meant to teach you. Pain is a great motivator. In fact, the two great motivators in your life are pain and pleasure. The more pain you experience, the more you're going to try to make that pain disappear. Some people do that through numbing, but the smart ones see the consequences as gifts, meant to show them something they never saw before. Perhaps that consequence will create a new action plan where the return is more pleasure than pain. Or maybe we go right back to our old ways, built-in trauma, and bullshit lies we've told ourselves and we get to deal with that same problem again. Because our problems sure don't run from us.

I have a friend and mentor who's a Realtor in California. Anni Dayan is an incredible human being. She made it her goal in 2020, when she saw people struggling, to give as much love in as many ways as possible. Each day she'd put money in the mailboxes of people she knew needed it. She'd show up and listen to people who were hurting. She'd ding-dong ditch her neighbors and leave them special treats. She did everything she could that year to make people smile. She sought out ways to love people, and she will tell you that her heart is full of more love now than ever. What you put out is what you get back.

I would be remiss if I didn't talk about self-talk as it relates to the law of cause and effect. The things you say to yourself, your mind hears. It never forgets. It *never* forgets anything. It's always stored in there. Everything you have ever experienced in your life is in the vault in your mind. You can't always retrieve it, which is why we so often don't understand our own reactions, triggers, or choices. *Why did I do that?* I have asked myself thousands of times. And most of the answers point the finger right back at myself. If the way you talk to yourself sucks, your life is going to feel that way. If you sit around telling yourself you're ugly, fat, not enough, tired, run-down, not happy, not fulfilled, not productive, or poor, for example—take a guess at what kind of things might be coming back your way. The vibration and energy of your thoughts and feelings will circle back around to you.

THE UNIVERSAL LAW OF ATTRACTION

This is perhaps one of the most well-known universal laws. There have been full books written on this topic, and I highly recommend you seek them out if you struggle in this area. You know the saying, "You're only as good as the people you hang out with"? Yeah, that's based on the universal law of attraction. It basically means that like attracts like. If you're a real asshole, chances are good that you hang out with real assholes. Because I've got to tell you, most high-quality and high-performing individuals aren't spending their free time and energy with someone who can't wait to ruin someone else's night. We already know that those people's inner worlds are just reflecting outward and we're seeing, in physical form, how they feel inside.

If you're funny, you probably attract funny people. If you're compassionate at your core, you're going to probably have a friend group of people with high levels of compassion. If you value family and relationships, you probably attract those people. In other words, you are what you attract. And also, this is a good time to remember that you are not what you detract. So, when you have the notion to get all up in your feelings about who's not following you or who has an issue with you, remember that they're pulling away from you for a reason, and that reason is not your issue, it's theirs. Take constructive feedback from people who know you, love you, and clearly want the best for you. Take constructive feedback from the people who have gone before you and are willing to give you their time and energy. Never take feedback from people who are determined not to like you because of your differences.

Be the person you want to attract. Recently I noticed that with very little exception, those in my friend group have a commonality I didn't always see. For the most part, we all have really great marriages. Not just good and surviving, but really close and thriving marriages. It's important to most of the people I spend my time with. And that makes sense because my marriage is so high on my priority and value list. It's proof that I'm attracting the things I actually care about into my life in the form of the people I know and love.

If you look at your circle of friends and relationships, what do you see? A bunch of people making decisions that are destructive? Any abuse? How about insecurity? Are you seeing people who are quiet and afraid to speak up about what they believe in? Do you share values with them, or do you find yourself having complaints about the relationship? Are you seeing friends in your group who make you a priority? Are they busy? How old are they? What do they have in common? What themes have you noticed come up regularly in your conversations?

If it's not what you'd like to see, the problem isn't your friend, it's you. Oh, snap!

You better get to work on figuring out what energy you're putting out into the world that is bringing behavior you don't value back to you. It's not enough to just wish for high-quality friends. You can't just hope you'll get them or visualize them into your life. Sure, those are parts of attracting things into your life, but you have to become the energy you want to receive. Want better friends? Be a better friend. Want people to teach you in your friend group? Better get to creating connections and teaching what you know. The more I teach, the more teachers find me. It's absolutely incredible how palpable this law is in my life.

We are designed to evolve. We are designed to try things and make preferences about them. We're created to change as we become wiser and learn the things we never knew. I hope nobody ever says of me, "She was steady as a rock and always had her shit together." No way, not me. If I'm not messing things up, I'm not pushing. If I'm not changing my mind, I'm not learning. If I'm not running into brick walls, it's because I'm not moving. Those are fear-based problems, and I will not have a fear-based problem that persists.

> **If I'm not messing things up, I'm not pushing. If I'm not changing my mind, I'm not learning. If I'm not running into brick walls, it's because I'm not moving.**

My best friend in the world bought a horse this week. Two months ago, she looked me straight in the eyes and said, "I will never buy a horse." That's what I'm talking about. Change your mind as you get new information. You never know what kind of trouble it could get you into. But at least you went for it. Those are the people I want in my life. What about you?

One final thing about the law of attraction. I want you to hear this one really clearly because it has affected me profoundly. My counselor once told me, "Lindsay, what you fear, you draw near." And dammit, he is right. If you're sitting around dwelling on the thing you're most afraid of, that thing is guaranteed to show up at your doorstep to have some dinner with you before it kicks you in the teeth. What you put your energy into is what you manifest. Your fears are powerful, and they are low-vibrational energies that attract, you guessed it, low-vibrational energies.

Let's make up a character as an example. Let's imagine a woman with low self-worth. She's beautiful, she's funny, she brings a lot to the table, but it seems that everyone can see that but her. She has a husband whom she loves, but she feels like she doesn't deserve him. She hides her body and her true self from her husband because she's embarrassed of what she brings to the table in those areas. She feels insane jealousy any time her husband leaves the house because she's sure he's going to find someone new and better than her to take her place. *How could he not?* she thinks.

This thought that she's turned into a fact in her mind is created out of fear. That fear can become so big and so loud in her mind that she begins to act out of that fear. She may start telling her husband about her jealousy. She may start accusing him of things he's never even thought of doing before. She may start telling her friends and loved ones about her negative feelings. She may push him away out of her fear for so long that eventually the thing she feared in her life, her husband cheating on her, can easily become a reality. What you believe about the world and yourself, your mind will set out to make come true. The thing you fear you will draw near.

> What you believe about the world and yourself, your mind will set out to make come true.

If you're sure you aren't worthy of a faithful and loving husband, then you aren't. That reality exists because you set your intentions on it. You are always manifesting the things you think about. Negative thoughts produce negative results. But the opposite is also true; positive thoughts produce positive results. If you love yourself like crazy and know you're worth a relationship that values you like the royalty you are, that's exactly what you'll find showing up for you.

Stop wasting your time on fear. Notice it. Think about what it could be here to teach you. Thank it for opening your eyes, and tell it to go. Interrupt the fear pattern you have going on in your mind by listing three things you're grateful for in that moment. It doesn't have to be related to your fear—just any three things to get your mind in a new pattern of gratitude. And then start taking action or sending your energy to what you do want in your life. Become that and watch your entire life change.

THE UNIVERSAL LAW OF COMPENSATION

The universal law of compensation simply states that what you give to others is what you receive in return. You will be compensated for exactly what you deserve in your life, big, small, and everything in between. You may be compensated in your life in many ways, through friendships, money, power, opportunities, and experiences.

This law is similar to the law of cause and effect, the difference being that the law of compensation states that any punishment or reward that you receive in your life is exactly what is deserved.

I was on the way to the airport with a family member a few years ago. On the drive there we passed through a quaint little neighborhood. One of the houses had a giant workshop adjacent to the house. It was filled with classic cars and a wall full of tools and gadgets. It was a beautiful place, and we began talking about it in the car because Michael really wants a classic car someday. "Yeah, but I wonder who they had to screw over or what they did to get something like that," slipped so easily from her mouth.

It's easy to assume that the people who have the things we want don't deserve them. Surely we deserve them. It's easy to convince ourselves that they have what we don't because they were willing to do something sinister and we would never do something like that. But we don't know that any of that is true. The truth is, we will be compensated in our lives based completely on what is deserved.

THE UNIVERSAL LAW OF PERPETUAL TRANSMUTATION OF ENERGY

Say that five times fast.

> You can change your life conditions, mindset, direction, or path right this second if you decide to.

The universal law of perpetual transmutation of energy (ULPTE for short because mouthful, amiright?) explains that every person has the ability to change their life at any moment. You can change your life conditions, mindset, direction, or path right this second if you decide to, and here's why. We, as humans, have the ability to change our vibration. Not only that, but our higher-vibrational frequencies will actually consume the lower-vibrational energies. Let me explain that a little more and give you a couple of examples.

It's been said that "everything is energy and that's all there is to it. Match the frequency of the reality you want, and you cannot help but get that reality. It can be no other way. This is physics."[4] What this means is that our emotions, thoughts, feelings, and decisions have a vibrational frequency. If you choose to interact with or act during low-vibrational thoughts (long wavelengths when measured) like fear, regret, sadness, or self-loathing, you will produce more of the same. If, however, you choose to interact with or act during high-vibrational thoughts (short wavelengths when measured) like love, peace, connectedness, and gratitude, you will experience more of the same.

Here's the greatest part of understanding that. Your high-vibrational energies will actually consume your low vibrations. The light is more powerful than the dark. If you're in a dark place, you have the ability to calm your mind, focus on what it is you do want, and seek something new from a high-vibrational place.

I used to consider myself a pessimist because I heard someone say that about my mom once when I was younger, and she and I shared a lot of similar personality traits. You'd be shocked by a lot of the stuff I believed about myself because someone told me; I really have come a long way on this path to fulfillment. Because I believed that and I told myself that, guess what my mind believed? Exactly. It believed what I told it, just like your mind will. From that place of pessimism, high-vibrational success like unconditional love and genuine community with others was not what I attracted even though it was the desire of my heart. The only thing I changed in my thirties when I started getting what I actually wanted out of my financial and work life was my awareness and thoughts of gratitude.

I have learned to interrupt low-vibrational thoughts and feelings by becoming aware of them when I'm thinking or feeling them. I simply stop the thought as soon as I recognize it by immediately listing to myself three things I'm grateful for in my life. As I mentioned earlier, they don't have to be linked to what you're dealing with. Just pick any three things that come to your mind that you're grateful for. That will interrupt your pattern of thinking, which we all fall victim to because it's how we're made. It will insert high-vibrational energy into your thoughts, and you'll be able to redirect your mind to attract or connect with the thoughts, feelings, outcomes, successes, and emotions you want more of in your life.

The ULPTE gives you the personal power to manifest anything into your life. Awareness of the vibrations you desire is so important. If what you want is a friend group that goes on adventures together, simply match the vibration of what you want. Start saying out loud that you are an amazing friend. Tell people what you want. Get excited and make plans for what you will do when you have it. Start getting together with some friends you know in different groups and see if they vibe together. You are in charge here!

THE UNIVERSAL LAW OF RELATIVITY

The universal law of relativity, put simply, says that each roadblock, obstacle, or problem that you face in your life is an opportunity to improve yourself. In essence, each dead end or frustration you feel is a door you can walk through to level up. This law demonstrates why it's so important not to numb ourselves to the things that feel uncomfortable. Let me give you an example.

Let's say you've decided you need to get your health in check, and one of the ways you're going to do that is through outdoor hiking. The first time you get to that mountain and start up, your mind is going to get uncomfortable. It's going to start pulling the *Maybe you should slow down* talk and giving you options to quit and come again another day. The more you push, the more uncomfortable you'll become and the louder your mind will get. Your mind is trying to keep you safe, and this hiking business doesn't seem safe.

Hiking is new for you, you're huffing and puffing, you slipped a little way back on the trail, and dang it's hot out right now—*This is stupid*, your mind may bark at you. But you push and you make it to the top. The next time you hit that trail, the experience will be a little different. It won't be quite as hard. Your mind will relax because you've done this before, and it can make correlations to the past when you remained safe. You've just leveled up. It may be incremental at first, but soon you won't hear the same discouragement up the mountain; you'll reach the top and realize you forgot how you got there because you were so deep in other thoughts.

I want you to insert the thing you're avoiding right now in place of the mountain in this story. Maybe it's going to the dentist because you're scared, like me. Maybe it's playing with your kids for a few hours every week because it feels weird. Perhaps it's being intimate with your spouse because you have some body image hang-ups. Whatever it is, you have the power to overcome and become a stronger and more powerful person than you were the day before. The universal law of relativity is here to guarantee you that the tough stuff is for you. You're going to hear me say that again and again in this book. Every roadblock is working for your betterment and not to crush you under its weight.

THE UNIVERSAL LAW OF POLARITY

This is one of my favorite laws to help me quickly change my mindset when I find myself struggling. I'm so grateful for what I've learned through this law in my life in the last two years. This law states that everything has an opposite and that without one you can never have the other. Without black, there would be no white. Without yin there would be no yang. You get the point.

You can actually change your thoughts by understanding this rule. If you're feeling sad, you can feed your mind the opposite thing to neutralize the thoughts or ideas that aren't working toward your highest good. Go read a book if it makes you happy when you're feeling sad. It helps. Go fill your belly when you're feeling hungry. Go call a friend if you feel lonely. That makes sense.

The way it's been the biggest blessing to me is to quell my fears, which can get pretty loud if I'm unaware of them. Here's an example from a counseling session that both Michael and I were in together. Michael is a vigilant person. He's an Enneagram six, *the loyalist.* He is constantly aware of his surroundings. I tell him all the time he'd be an amazing detective. Nothing gets past him when it comes to details. And all of this information he puts in his brain, his ego tells him helps him control his world.

Naturally, with three daughters, Michael is protective. Up until last year, I'd have said "overprotective" in the way that he thought he could always keep them safe from hurt or harm or danger or sadness or all of the things he perceived as "bad." And every time he overprotected them, he stole their moment to learn. At times, this has caused disagreement in our marriage as far as how we want to raise our daughters.

Here's where this law becomes a super handy tool to have in your arsenal. We all tend to focus on the negative results of what we perceive are problems in our life. If you were asking Michael about all the bad things that could happen to his kids without him there to protect and watch over them, he would have rattled them off for you in minutes because he thought about them all the time. Of course, he was doing that because he loves his daughters so much he never wants them to hurt, which is not reality and it's based in 100 percent fantasy land. *I don't want them to get pregnant in high school. I don't want them to fight over a boy. I don't want them to be abused by someone. I don't want them to screw up their life by making dumb decisions, so I need to help them.* But he was only seeing the negative consequences to the girls' actions, and never the positive.

For every negative there is a positive. In fact, for every single negative, there is a positive. If our daughter Teagan decided to have sex in high school with a dude who didn't really like her and then he left her pregnant and alone, most of us would see that as a real shitty situation for her. But in reality, it's equally negative and positive. Oh, you got jokes, Lindsay! Hear me out. This situation doesn't come with a label; it is reality, and it is for her as long as she chooses to see this difficult situation as such. And the same goes for us as her parents. It's not our lesson to take from her.

We can guide her, we can talk to her about how her actions may affect her, but we cannot control her. Her actions and decisions are hers. And what if she did end up there? What possible things might come of that? Michael and I get to become young grandparents with amazing energy. We get to be there to support our daughter through pregnancy in a very intimate way. Teagan learns early about her priorities in life. She experiences love in a new way that many her age don't experience.

When something you perceive as negative lands in your lap, you have a choice. You can focus on all the really crappy things you'll have to experience, or you can focus on why it's the best thing that ever happened. I know a lot of moms who had kids in high school, and while most of them wouldn't call it ideal, they all say it was the best thing that ever happened to them. I can look back on all the things I thought were terrible in my life and I know that the growth was worth the challenge—that just because it was harder doesn't make it bad. There is no bad and there is no good. There is only what is. Nothing is ever all one way or the other.

> **There is no bad and there is no good. There is only what is.**

THE UNIVERSAL LAW OF RHYTHM

You've likely been introduced to the circadian rhythm. Circadian rhythms are twenty-four-hour cycles of physical, mental, and behavioral changes. Wake, work, wind down, sleep, and then you do it all over again the next day. It's a pattern that our planet and living beings follow. When I travel internationally, I find the disruption in this pattern to be incredibly difficult on my mind, body, and sleep patterns, that's how connected to the circadian rhythm I am. Jetlag is no joke, and if you've ever had to perform after an international flight, you know that foggy-brained, what-is-even-happening-right-now feeling.

Not only do we have daily patterns, but our seasons come and go in predictable patterns as well. We are wired to follow patterns, and our mind works to put us into those patterns so our environment is more predictable. We have routines that follow a rhythm. Our bodies follow a rhythm every month (or so); women are keenly aware of that fact. Our emotions also follow a pattern. Have you ever noticed your emotional pattern?

Recently a friend of mine who is an expert in human design, Rosy Crescitelli, helped me become aware of my emotional patterns. On any given month I may have days where everything is sunny and happy, and I'll have days where I'm inexplicably low energy or tense inside. I used to think my sunny days were how I was supposed to feel every day, so I would become frustrated by the lows. I have come to understand that we all have patterns of lows and highs in a given week or month. As you flow in and out of the lows and highs, it's a good idea to track your pattern so you can become more aware of how your body and mind work because it can be a great advantage for you.

Side note: there are some amazing apps to help you track your mood throughout the day, and they will send you reports with all of that information compiled if you'd like to find your patterns. Many of those apps will send you push notifications with a quick check-in throughout the day as many times as you'd like. Because tech changes so fast, I'm not going to list them here, but a quick search of the internet for mood-tracking apps will give you plenty of options so you can choose the right one for you.

In the past couple of years, I've started waiting on decision-making until I've gone through a complete emotional cycle. Before I decide if something is serving my highest good or not, I feel it through the lows and the highs that inevitably follow. Mine generally last anywhere from two to five days and have become quite predictable. I'll usually know it's going to be one of those low-frequency days when I wake up tired, lethargic, concerned about something, worried, or generally feeling annoyed. When it's going to be a happy, normal day, I'll feel the opposite. I'll wake up with joy, looking forward to my morning coffee, smiling with my husband, and feeling ready for my day. It's kind of like waking up excited for your morning coffee versus waking up saying, "I really need a cup of coffee to get through this day." What a gift it is to understand that sometimes my lows are meant for me to evaluate a choice or decision through both a low-vibrational and high-vibrational energy.

Here's how this looks when I use it properly:

A couple of years ago, Michael and I were presented with an opportunity to buy a business that was struggling financially. We knew the business had potential to be profitable and that the previous owners had not run it in a way that would sustain it in the future without a complete overhaul. Because Michael and I run our businesses in the black, meaning out of debt, it was a struggle to make the decision to move forward. We intentionally sat with the opportunity for longer than a few days when we were excited about the opportunity.

I needed to feel what that business would feel like on my shoulders when I wasn't in a good, shiny, happy place. How would it feel to have the responsibility for that debt when I was feeling down? Did it feel right still? Would I be proud of my choice, or would I have second thoughts? Michael and I both did the same thing, and we continued to check in with each other with how we were feeling through the highs and the lows that came for both of us. It inspired a game plan for that business that allowed us to get it out of debt and into profits in less than six months. Our confidence for that project was born of patience, delayed gratification, and trust that we were equipped for the job.

I make better decisions when I see something from more than one side and in more than one state of mind. I like to trust my gut for most small decisions like picking my cabinet colors or choosing an outfit, so don't misunderstand me about what requires a few days to think over. I don't waste time going back and forth on things that are really inconsequential when it comes to my fulfillment. However, making big choices with large impact when I'm feeling happy is very different from making choices when I'm sad. I don't want my emotions dictating what I pursue in my life, so I became aware of my rhythms.

It's important that you don't fight against your natural rhythm. Work with it. If your cycle is telling you to rest, make rest a priority. Listen to your body; it's trying to communicate with you. If your body is telling

Victimhood will not push you toward true fulfillment.

you to push, do it. Follow your rhythm and allow what comes with it to flow through you. Be careful not to fall into the trap of defining your life by the low moments. As I mentioned previously, victimhood will not push you toward true fulfillment. You don't need someone to feel sympathy for you, because each of your bad days was working in your best interests to make you who you are today—a stronger and more equipped version of you.

THE UNIVERSAL LAW OF GENDER

This law has less to do with your gender and more to do with the "feminine" and "masculine" energy in all things. The masculine energy has a lot of "doing" in it and the feminine has a lot of "nurturing" in it. Each of us has both masculine and feminine energies in us that help us experience the world and grow. You may notice that you tend to display more masculine energy than feminine or vice versa, but you will still display both at different times in your life.

Masculine energy is usually associated with diligence, hustle, structure, organization, motivation, and decisiveness, while feminine energy is associated with inspiration, empathy, intuition, imagination, gentleness, and compassion. Not all females work in the feminine energy, and not all males work in the masculine energy.

I find that when I'm in go mode, I tend to make most of my decisions from the masculine side of me. That can make me overly analytical and critical. It can make me self-sabotage at times, and I can become dominating about the way I think things should be done. When I left my house at eighteen, I believed that I had to display a tougher energy to survive based on what I was taught. My mom had very masculine energy during my childhood out of her own need to survive. As I've grown, I've started to embrace my feminine side instead of hiding it behind a wall to protect my feelings and my heart. Feminine energy tends to be a bit more vulnerable for me, so I have kept it hidden away like my ego told me to. *Don't let them see you cry. Never let them see you sweat. Don't talk about your feelings.* Those are all ways I've denied my feminine side, and it has never worked to serve my highest good. Trying to control my masculine and feminine sides without allowing them to serve me has landed me in hot water in all areas of my life.

Too much masculine energy can make you cold and dominating. Too much feminine energy can make you become a doormat for others to walk on. Not enough masculine energy could be responsible for your feelings of low self-worth or lack of motivation. With not enough feminine energy, you might find yourself feeling hollow or emotionally unavailable.

You can harness the power of your masculine and feminine sides to help you reach fulfillment. Becoming connected to the side of you that you feel most comfortable displaying will help you feel more authentic and fulfilled when you get it. There is no winner here. Masculine and feminine are both great qualities. What you really want to do is figure out which energy you act out of the most. A quick way to determine which side of your personality you're working out of is to ask yourself this question: Do you have a desire to do the taking or to be taken when you're being intimate? Yeah, that's pretty much an animal instinct. It won't be all the time and there are exceptions, but in general, if you want to be the dominant one with your partner, you're acting from your masculine energy. If you want to be told what to do in those situations, it's probable that you're acting out of your feminine energy.

As someone who can easily slip into both (chameleon, remember?), I have to be extra careful to hold back the side I push forward out of fear, which is my masculine energy. I have found ways to become that "gentle giant," displaying both masculine and feminine in ways that help me reach my goals and dreams but in a way that's not threatening. Allow yourself to see your decisions in meditation as you see them with both your masculine and feminine sides.

As I've become friends with my feminine side and realized she's not here to allow me to be hurt all the time, the more me I feel. The less I deny parts of me that are real, the more grounded and fulfilled I feel. Make peace with both sides and call on both sides when you need them. They're meant to serve you, not define you.

Once I started to understand the twelve universal laws, I started seeing almost everything in my life differently. Things that used to send me into a tailspin now wake me up to pay attention. The things that used to make me sad I see differently now. The things that used to make me angry still do at times, but I can use that anger to inspire change. And if it's not of enough importance to take action on, it's not important enough to take up the precious minutes in my life.

I'm nowhere near perfect. I struggle every single day to thank my former self for protecting me as a child and then choosing to think differently and act differently. Just like all long-term change, it can often feel like a two-steps-forward-and-one-step-back situation. This was never supposed to be an easy road. It was supposed to challenge the hell out of us, and we were meant to rise to that challenge. As the months pass, living up to my true potential becomes noticeably easier if I take the time to notice.

Use the twelve laws to help reframe your mindset and set yourself free, because freedom to be who you were created to be is required to fly. This information coupled with the information you're about to discover about your values is going to set you up for huge success in the second part of this book, where we actually put the information to use.

OUR VALUES

★ ★ ★ ★ ★ ★ ★ ★ ★

KEEP US ON THE RIGHT ROADS

★ ★ ★ ★ ★ ★ ★ ★ ★

IN OUR LIVES

VALUES

I don't believe in motivation. I believe that we each have different values in our lives, the kinds of values that connect us to each of the cornerstones of a good life. We let those values dictate where we spend our time and resources. It is my belief that God has created us with unique values and desires us to create a life that looks unlike any other on earth.

I like to think of our values as street signs along the road. As you're driving down the road of your life, you'll pass signs along the way that tell you you're on the right path. If you start feeling a little lost and you look for signs but you're not seeing any, there's a good chance you got off on the wrong exit somewhere. Our values keep us on the right roads in our lives. Your values offer you clues that even though you've never driven here before, you're right where you're supposed to be.

> It is my belief that God has created us with unique values.

Last year, I sat with my therapist and went through my list of values, something we're going to do together shortly. When all was said and done, he said, "I can't help but notice that you're not on this list. And I don't mean in some ways; I mean you are not on this list at all. How does that make you feel?" And it didn't make me feel weird, you guys. I didn't feel any kind of way about it. It just was. My work was all over it, my kids and my husband were on there, travel was on there, but I was nowhere to be seen. The only way I was taking care of me was when I was numbing in front of a TV or eating a Reese's Peanut Butter Cup with the tiny little Reese's Pieces inside. (Have you had those? Wow. They taste like rainbows exploding in your mouth.) I had, without even trying or thinking about it, made everything else a priority but myself. And the craziest part is that it wasn't so much that I made everyone else a priority over myself, it was that I didn't want to think about myself. At all. It's easier to solve other people's problems, and to be honest, I'm pretty good at it. So it makes sense I didn't want any part of getting into the gym to voluntarily hurt myself every day. Sweating was a *No* for me, dawg. And taking care of my emotions, feelings, and general well-being felt like fluff. Something had to change.

This year, when I finally, after thirty-nine years, put my name on that list of values, it meant a year of possibly the hardest work I've ever done on myself. I fought it. For two months following that values exercise, I thought of ways to make myself follow through with some self-care. And one day I realized that the motivation I was waiting for was never going to come. I was going to have to make myself. It was either I make myself try or I find myself in the same unhealthy situation next year, and I truly wanted better. I truly wanted to feel fulfilled in the body my soul walks around in. I bought a yoga mat and let it sit in my room for a month, and then one day I went out into the sun and I made myself do an online yoga class. One high-vibrational decision begets another one. Remember our high vibes consume the low ones. The more I did it, the better I felt. It was never easier, I just kept getting better.

Last year I took four hundred Peloton classes. I started cooking meals to nourish my body and not to satisfy my addictions to sugar and entire loaves of bread. I began reading studies about the chemicals in our water like fluoride as it connects to our brain function—specifically, how it connects to the pineal gland, where our intuition comes from. I began addressing the relationship I have with my tween daughters. I started addressing the baggage I brought into my marriage by being insanely honest about everything and keeping almost nothing hidden inside. I began reevaluating our healthcare methods. I began seeking out ways to learn new skills that would help me live longer and more efficiently. I began setting hard boundaries around my time, without fear about how that will make others feel. I began letting myself off the hook for the mistakes I made (some on purpose). I forgave myself. I wiped the slate clean and went to work on connecting with my spirit.

Values help you determine what you stand for or what's most important to you in your life. Values are a part of your spirit. They're what make you *you*. Fulfillment comes when you work toward the things you value highly in the way that is true to those same values. Your values aren't your needs; they're your compass that points to your true north—your fulfillment. Your personal values will help you focus on your vision, your idea of a "good life," by showing you if you're on or off the path, just as a compass would if you were hiking in the forest without a map.

Before we get to the exercise to help you discover or reacquaint yourself with your values, I want one thing from you. I want you to promise yourself that you will answer the questions honestly and authentically. When you break a promise to yourself, your mind never forgets it, and I guarantee you it will serve it up to you when you're going through something hard. The more promises you keep, the more promises you will keep. It's an upward spiral.

VALUES EXERCISE

Inherited values are values passed down to us through our culture, society, social norms, family, religion, and genetics. Our inherited values often have a huge influence on our core values, and that's okay. But the problem is when we passively believe our inherited values are who we are, and that they are by default our core values, just because we are told they should be. The way to reach self-actualization and a life of fulfillment is by questioning everything we have been taught to believe. You may find that your cultural and personal values overlap. Excellent. But maybe they don't, and that's an excellent discovery as well. Not every inherited value is wrong. But we do need to look at how we spend our time, money, and resources and make sure the values that those actions align with are actually what we value in our core. We need to do that values assessment to figure out what is true to us and what was given to us through outside sources.

In 1992, Shalom Schwartz created the Schwartz theory of basic values.[1] Schwartz conducted a wide survey of over 60,000 participants to identify the guiding principles in a person's life. He was able to drill all of the data into ten value types, and I have found them to be really fascinating. I've listed the core values below. Additionally, I've given a short definition and common traits you may see in connection with each core value to help you understand them a bit more.

BENEVOLENCE

Meaning: Having a disposition to do something good, kind, or charitable for the advancement of others, especially family

Traits: Empathetic, helpful, honest, forgiving, responsible, friendly, accountable

UNIVERSALISM

Meaning: Desiring to understand, feel appreciation for, and protect the welfare of both nature and all other people

Traits: Open-minded; interested in social justice, equality, the world at peace, the world of beauty, unity with nature, wisdom, and protecting the environment

SELF-DIRECTION

Meaning: Independent choice, thought, action, creation, and exploration

Traits: Creative, free, showing willpower, curious, independent, self-disciplined

SECURITY

Meaning: Stability and safety of society, of relationships, and of self

Traits: Valuing social order, financial security, family safety, and sense of belonging; clean, consistent, healthy, thorough

CONFORMITY

Meaning: Restraint of actions, predispositions, and desires likely to disrupt norms or upset others

Traits: Obedient, self-disciplined, loyal, polite, honoring parents, respecting elders

HEDONISM

Meaning: Pursuit of pleasure as the highest good

Traits: Valuing fun, pleasure, self-indulgence, amusement, and enthusiasm; enjoying life

ACHIEVEMENT

Meaning: Success through personal accomplishment

Traits: Ambitious, results-oriented, capable, influential, determined, powerful, successful

TRADITION

Meaning: Respect, commitment, and acceptance of long-standing cultural and religious customs and practices

Traits: Respecting tradition, humble, devout, ritualistic, accepting of what is given

STIMULATION

Meaning: Enthusiasm, uniqueness, excitement, and challenges in life

Traits: Valuing variation, having an exciting life, daring, brave, driven, energetic

POWER

Meaning: Control over themselves, others, and resources; social status and prestige

Traits: Influential, in authority, wealthy, socially powerful, respected, socially recognized

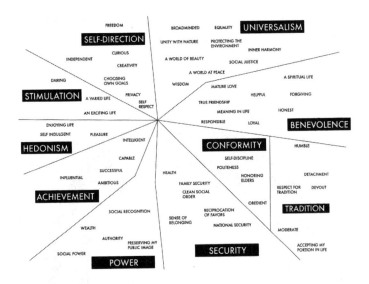

Attaining values outside of what's important to you specifically will not bring you happiness.

You'll notice that happiness and fulfillment are surprisingly missing from the list of values and from the expressions of those values. That's because happiness and fulfillment are derived from attaining your values. Attaining values outside of what's important to you specifically will not bring you happiness. This is why it never works to morph yourself into the goals and plans of someone else.

What brings them happiness and value will not do the same for you, and vice versa.

Narrowing down the things you actually value will help you understand and know yourself so much better. These little clues about how you behave will help you be in control of your mind rather than the other way around. Remember, most people are not aware of the reasons they behave in certain ways or why they find themselves in the same situation over and over again. Your simply being aware is going to be a huge advantage when you start moving into action.

These values and how important they are to you can help you understand the drivers to your behavior and motivation. I know because when I work in my values, I don't have to worry about motivating myself. Most of this process is less about discovering something new about yourself and more about understanding who you are at your core, who you were

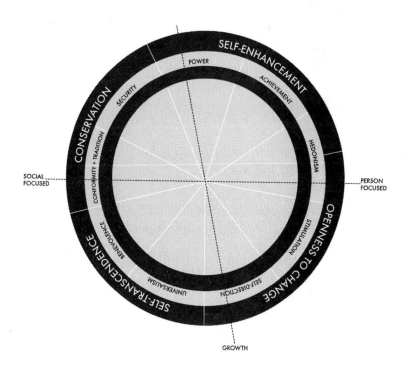

created to be, who you evolved into, and how your past traumas and joys have affected the way you behave.

The image above offers another revealing vantage point when looking at values. Each side of the circle represents a dichotomy between person-focused and social-focused values and the same between protection and growth. If you're a person who values safety and protection, it makes sense that the deeper you are into protecting yourself or your way of life, the less life growth you'll be focused on getting because you can't do both 100 percent of the time. Growth usually doesn't feel safe, in my experience. There's inherent risk in growth because the unknown is risky.

Take a look at this list and rank each value category from highest priority to lowest, one being the most important to you and ten being the least.

Benevolence
Universalism
Self-direction
Security
Conformity
Hedonism
Achievement
Tradition
Stimulation
Power

As you walk through the list, do your best to rank each value in order of importance based on the meaning and traits outlined for each one on pages 68–70. Remember that nobody is going to see this list. Don't list benevolence as your highest value because you believe it might make you look more noble to others or because you have some incorrect notion that one value is more desirable than the other. We need you just the way you are. In the same sense, there's no reason to list self-direction as your highest value if you know you're more prone to success when you work with a group of people. No one value is better than the others. You're entering the no-judgment zone. Welcome, it's super fun in here!

1. _____
2. _____
3. _____
4. _____
5. _____
6. _____
7. _____
8. _____
9. _____
10. _____

If you're having a hard time figuring out which values are the most important to you, I have some questions for you that might help narrow it down.

1. When was the last time you felt yourself in flow? You were working hard but it felt so good to you on the inside. You were happy. You found yourself smiling. You were satisfied at the end of the day. Where were you? What were you doing? What values were you displaying at that time?

2. When was the last time you became completely flustered or frustrated by an activity or an obligation? You couldn't wait until it was over. It wasn't a great experience. You don't want to go do that again. Where were you? What were you doing? What values were you displaying at the time? It is likely that what you were doing was in conflict with one of your actual core values.

3. What values are "built into your DNA"? These are the kinds of things you believe you were born with. The kinds of things that you must have or refuse to have in your life to feel fulfilled on a daily basis. Don't forget to take those things into consideration.

The clarity gained from doing this exercise is foundational for the next steps in this process. As you build your life, piece by piece, this will bring insight to you when it comes to what you care about most. Now that we've covered values, let's go meet some goals. You've got this.

I CHALLENGE YOU TO **LOOK UP** FROM THE GRAVE EVERYDAY

THE WOOP EXPERIENCE

There are a lot of methods to help you meet your goals: little tips and tricks that promise to give you a better chance at success, and most of them will work—for a time. Many of them are checklists of sorts to help you get on the right path, but they don't help you to actually use your mind and body to create change. I want to fix that. I want to give you a method for change that will direct you through some activities that make staying the same a whole lot more difficult. I want to make staying the same so difficult for you that the action of change feels like a cool breeze on a swelteringly hot summer afternoon in the Arizona desert. I want action to be that cold glass of ice water you drink every day because you need it, not because you want it. The method I've found to do that is called the WOOP (there it is), originally developed using twenty years of research on motivation by Gabriele Oettingen.[1] For the purposes of our wake-up work, we're going to use the WOOP framework, and I'm going to give you some activities, ideas, and exercises to do within each one.

WOOP stands for wish, outcome, obstacle, and plan.

WOOP sounds simple, I know, but it's not going to be some easy activity you do for a few minutes one day and then never think about again. I'm going to show you how to integrate the tools you will learn into the WOOP experience so that you have a full, immersive experience from the initial desire to the action you take to make that desire a reality. It's going to take time and it's going to be worth it if what you really desire is change. You can't kinda want it. You can't maybe someday want it. You can't hold on to the old and desire the new at the same time. You have to commit. If you take the time to walk through this WOOP experience, it's going to change the way you think and it's going to change the energy you're putting out into the world.

WISH

This is the part of the experience where you allow yourself to dream. This is where you sit in the things you want and decide if they're going to be worth the work it will take to get there. For this first run-through of the WOOP experience, I want you to choose just one thing you want in your life. Choose one thing that seems to be missing. Choose one thing that you know you should do, learn, become, or pursue but haven't yet. Choose the thing you procrastinate on. Choose the thing you're really afraid of but would be so excited to accomplish. Choose just one thing you wish for and write it here:

I wish _____

_____

The first wish I ever had when I did this experience was to work out regularly. That's it. I wanted to work out regularly. Your wish doesn't have to be complicated; it just has to be something you want that has so far eluded you in life.

There are two parts to the wish component of the WOOP experience:

1. Contemplate your death.
2. Desire change.

WISH PART 1: CONTEMPLATE YOUR DEATH

Let's take some time to imagine our deaths. *Oh, wait a minute. Did she just say death? That can't be right.* Yeah, that's right. Let's get our morbid on for a minute.

In order to know what you wish for, you need to have some perspective. Thinking about your death is going to give you that. If you want to live a good life, you have to plan your death. You have to acknowledge the fact that you are going to die. Assuming we're only here once, you've got one chance to see the things, learn the lessons, taste the food, smell the flowers, feel the feelings, find God, know yourself, and love others.

Think about your death. Imagine today is your last day. In the instant you read this, you ceased to exist in physical form on this earth. But your spirit hangs around to see what happens next. What do you regret? What do you wish you'd said? What do you wish you'd tried? What opportunities did you miss? What will the people around you say and mean about your life? How proud are you of what was produced with your time on earth?

Thinking about death, while unpleasant at times, is a great exercise for you to do daily. It can help you put small inconveniences and hurts into perspective and help you become more emotionally connected to taking care of yourself in every way. Thinking about death can help you reprioritize your values, goals, and desires for your life. And that's not just me saying that; that's science.

Researchers were able to connect thoughts or proximity to death and the act of helping others in a recent study.[2] In fact, people on the street who were within a block of a cemetery were 40 percent more likely to be of service to another human. Thinking about death can give us a more fulfilling and compassionate life. I challenge you to look up from your grave every day. Talk about a change in perspective.

None of us know how long we have. One of the greatest gifts of my life was losing my mom unexpectedly and without being able to say goodbye to her. I learned about death in a tangible way that day, and it has affected my life profoundly. I know my time could be up with no warning or reason at any time. I'm not fearful of death now like I was before that experience. You're bound to accomplish and enjoy more when you know it won't last forever—when you know there's limited time on earth to feel those feelings. I have become more grateful for what I feel and experience knowing that death is claiming every second that passes by. Thinking about death can put our life into perspective and help us focus on what really matters. It will also help you understand what you really want in your life. If you take everything away, even your life, what will you want the most?

> Thinking about death can put our life into perspective and help us focus on what really matters.

A few years ago, Michael and I took our kids on their first vacation overseas. We went to England and France for a couple of weeks in the summer to see the things they were learning about in school. On one of the days, we headed out to a small town in the English countryside on the way to Windsor Castle. There, we took archery lessons and practiced alongside some other families.

As entrepreneurs are wont to do, Michael started asking the couple who owned the archery school about how they got started and what their work schedule looked like. We love seeing people do something they're passionate about, and it was clear these two loved their lives and loved working with each other. The story Steve and Carol told us about how they got into their business was one of the most impactful stories I've ever heard and has stuck with both Michael and me over the years.

Years ago, Steve and Carol both worked in London in high-paying corporate jobs. Neither of them loved their job but they were golden-handcuffed to them and did their best to escape the city when they could. One year, they decided to take a vacation to Indonesia.

The couple boarded a ferry-style boat in Indonesia, where they were taking in the sights and enjoying their holiday. The vessel capacity was a total of just over two hundred, but the port authority later admitted to allowing more than capacity to board, because a giant floating vessel in open water isn't serious business, you know? With what is now believed to be over six hundred passengers on board, the boat sank in the ocean in the middle of the night.

Steve and Carol had no choice but to jump in the water and swim for shore, which was nowhere to be seen as they were seventy to seventy-five miles off of the coast at the time of the disaster. For hours they swam through the day and the night to try to stay alive without life jackets. Steve recalled that during the night the two would take turns exchanging stories about the things they'd do and the things they'd change when they were rescued. As he was treading water for hours on end, Steve said he was crying and begging God for one more day with his wife on earth. The two encouraged each other and continued pushing through the grueling physical and mental pain with thoughts about how their life would change the minute this was over. They were finally rescued by Indonesian authorities twenty hours after they initially hit the water and after having almost given up dozens of times.

Following that experience, Steve and Carol both quit their £100,000-per-year jobs, immediately having realized that you can't buy back time. Since that day, the two have been enjoying their lives by becoming entrepreneurs doing something they love, archery. They now work just five months out of the year and spend the other seven months traveling the world and soaking up all that life has to offer. Both will tell you that terrifying brush with death was the best thing that ever happened to them.

Wake up, your life is waiting for you to really live it! The boat has been overcrowded and you get to decide what to do next. Are you fighting, or drowning? What are you going to change when you decide to really live?

WISH PART 1: CONTEMPLATE YOUR DEATH (EXERCISE)

In this part of the experience, I want you to take the time to see yourself dead and looking up from your grave. Who is there? What is important at that moment? How will this desire you have for your life impact how you live up until your death? Thinking about your death will help you prioritize the things you want.

Let's imagine that you're in debt right now and you'd love the freedom and the feeling of being debt free. You know you need to get your finances in order. Your debt is a crushing source of stress in your life, but you don't know how to get your spending under control with all you have going on in your life right now. First, we need to think about this from a dead point of view—*I'll take "things you never thought you'd buy a book about" for $1,000, Alex.*

Seriously, I want you to imagine now that you're dead:

Has reaching this goal changed the way you lived your life?

Has it benefited you?

How has your being debt free affected the people who are at your funeral?

You're dead. Is having your finances in order important to you and the people who knew you?

Are your finances going to have to be a priority at one point in your life?

Thinking about your death in the WOOP experience will help you with the following:

1. It reveals your priorities.
2. It helps you feel unstuck by changing the patterns your mind so easily slips into.
3. It will help you focus on your life as a whole and not in parts.
4. It helps you delay gratification for your highest good.
5. It will help you focus on the present, knowing every moment that passes is claimed by death.
6. It will reveal the impact of small decisions now.

7. It minimizes your current emotions.

So think about your death and how this change you want to make (your wish) may impact the life you have left. Still worth it?

WISH PART 2: DESIRE CHANGE

Okay, now you need to admit that you have a desire for change. You have to say it (putting words into the open air actually stimulates your entire vibrational flow because speaking them gives them legit life to exist as those words run to action). You need to put out into your world that you want the change. Talk about it with your spouse or friends. Admit to yourself that giving up your old way is going to be a necessary change in your life. This is not a passive desire anymore; we're looking for an active desire for change here.

Admit to yourself that giving up your old way is going to be a necessary change in your life.

This step seems simple, I know, but your intentions will direct your mind on where to act and what to do next. Your intention for change will start attracting people and things into your life to help you achieve the change you desire. The desire for change gives me butterflies in my stomach sometimes because I know it means I'm about to experience the growth process. That butterflies feeling can be interpreted one of two ways: as excitement or as nervousness. You get to choose, but you can't experience both at the same time.

In the debt scenario we talked about in part 1, you may look to someone you know who has really done well in their finances as inspiration for change. You may look at their wealth and desire that feeling for yourself. You may imagine what it would feel like to be debt free and finally make the decision that the change is going to be worth the effort and sacrifices it will take to achieve being debt free. It may be that you want to teach your kids now the things you never learned growing up.

OUTCOME

This is the fun part where you get to imagine your life once you've actually achieved your goal. You get to sit in the feelings you'll feel when you're the person you're wanting to be. I like to think of this part as a little bit spiritual. Sit in the change you want and think about how your spirit will feel about your life at that point. Is this action taking you closer or further away from your highest self? Is this something your spirit needs in order to accomplish its purpose? Are the changes you're about to make in your life connecting you to your values? Imagine how amazing it will feel to live a life where your spirit, values, and actions are aligned.

There are two parts of the outcome portion of the WOOP experience:

1. Think from a spiritual perspective.
2. Connect with your values.

OUTCOME PART 1: THINK FROM A SPIRITUAL PERSPECTIVE

Our spirit is the part of us that connects to God. Our soul is the part of us that connects to our mind and body. Both are important, but I want you to connect your desired change for your life with your spirit. I want you to ask for clarity here. I want you and God to partner on this mission.

You were never meant to do this alone.

> I want you and God to partner on this mission. You were never meant to do this alone.

This is the part of the WOOP experience where you may find meditation or prayer a really powerful tool. Spiritually, from the part of you that is God-breathed, how will this change affect your calling or your purpose? If you aren't sure what your purpose is yet, that's okay. You don't need to know your purpose to know if the action is correct for you. There is a purpose for your life. You are being used as a tool for a story that is bigger than just you. You are here to profoundly affect others with your life. Will this change help you do that?

Let's go back to that debt scenario. Will being debt free allow you more freedom or ability to carry out your purpose? H&R Block recently released a study that showed that 59 percent of Americans worry about money "constantly."[3] Imagine you're one of them (and chances are good that you are, according to this statistic). Would taking that worry off of your plate help you see the other parts of your life differently? Would it free you up to carry out your spiritual purpose? Of course it would. We all have experienced constant worry at one time or another in our lives, and it is a very low-vibrational feeling. Constant worry will color the way you see the world. Connect your desire for change with your spirit and allow that feeling to soak into you. Having no debt in your life will give you the money you need to live a life of impact. Imagine what you could do with no debt and an account set aside for you to use toward your next goal. What a feeling of freedom and relief.

OUTCOME PART 2: CONNECT WITH YOUR VALUES

In the previous section we talked about your values and how to determine if something you're working on fits into those values. You never want to take action on an end result that you don't value. That's how you end up frustrated and angry. I don't want that for you. Can you connect the change you want to make in your life to moving you closer to something you value? How about figuring out how the change you want to make allows you to live out the things you value more?

Perhaps this one goal in your life will lead you to accomplishing the bigger plans God has for you. Connect your desires for your life to the things you value as a way to weed out the things that aren't actually for you and to give yourself assurance that the path you're on can lead you to a more fulfilling life. This right here is why it's so important to understand the things you value. Each and every action you take should get you closer to one of those things.

OBSTACLE

An obstacle is a roadblock on the way to success that you'll have to either maneuver around, over, or through. You can often see obstacles coming simply by connecting your current reality to your desired reality. The obstacles will come at you fast and furious as soon as you start putting your mind to work on getting what you want. Your mind probably went into overdrive telling you all the reasons you couldn't have that or didn't deserve the wish you wrote at the beginning of this chapter.

In this part of the WOOP experience, you're simply going to notice what the biggest obstacles are to your success. What can you see coming down the road that would threaten your ability to reach your goals? Who might not like the idea of you making changes right now? What kind of feedback are you bound to get from yourself and from others? How will this affect the amount of time you have for the other priorities in your life? What might you have to set down for a time in order to reach the success or fulfillment you're looking for in your life?

Here are a few things to consider when you start thinking about obstacles that you may have to face in the future.

1. Destructive habits or addictions
2. Common distractions
3. Fatigue
4. Fears
5. Negative people in your life
6. Your comfort
7. Self-doubt
8. Dreaming replacing action
9. Perfectionist tendencies
10. Quitting

Take the time to think through how some of these things could throw you off of your path and onto a path that seems so much easier and more exciting when things get tough. How might you combat and overcome these obstacles so they're only temporary setbacks and not your sign to up and walk away from your need for fulfillment? The first step when you have a problem is to admit that there's a problem. If you've seen any of these things mess up a goal you've had in the past, don't let them come in the way of this one. Learn from your past mistakes and make a plan for the obstacles.

PLAN

This is the part of the WOOP experience where we create breakthrough. This is the part where you finally feel that motivation or push to make change happen. I can physically feel this push in my body and in my mind. It's an amazing feeling. It's a feeling that many people think will stay with them. It will not. The feeling of motivation will come and go, just like all feelings.

This process you're about to learn is here for you to come back to any time you find yourself short on motivational feelings. And if it doesn't produce that, it will help you find the self-discipline necessary to do it anyway. Let's look at our debt-free example: you won't always feel motivated to make good financial choices on your road to becoming debt free, but this exercise will make it feel like less of a choice. This exercise will help convince your mind that you need these good choices to be fulfilled.

There are three parts to the planning portion of the WOOP experience:

1. Determine your action plan.
2. Connect pleasure and pain.
3. Go to work.

PLAN PART 1: DETERMINE YOUR ACTION PLAN

Within each of us is an ability to know what to do in any situation. Many of us don't trust the inner voice of our spirit. That spirit sometimes tells us to do crazy things that our mind cannot get on board with. Our spirit pushes us to want more and try harder. Our spirit encourages us to speak up and exist on purpose. Our spirit and our mind are often at war with one another. But the great news is that if you know what you want and you've completed the first three parts of the WOOP experience, your plan is simply waiting to be revealed to you. You simply need to ask yourself the question I first heard from Patti Dobrowolski during a conference: *What three things do I need to do right now to make the vision I have for my future a reality?*[4]

Ask yourself the question and then close your eyes and wait for the answers. You already have the answers in you. Notice you asked for more than one action you can take right now that is within your control. This allows there to be no excuse when you try once and you don't get the result you want. I'm trying my best to make sure you don't quit on yourself.

Let's imagine us in that debt scenario again. You really want to get out of debt. You have a family at home depending on you; you feel like you're doing everything in your power to bring in extra cash; you're living paycheck to paycheck. What three things do you need to do right now to make the vision you have for your financial future a reality?

First you ask, and then you listen.

Quiet your fears if they get loud by thinking about the things you're grateful for in your life. Center your thoughts and ask the question again.

What three things can you do right now to make the vision you have for your future a reality?

Don't be afraid to write down the answers you get, even if they seem really, really scary. Many of the actions you'll need to take will feel scary. That's *preeeeetty* much the point. You're strong enough to face even the scariest thing you can imagine if fulfillment is waiting on the other side. I think you'll find that overcoming fears and doubts is the fulfillment.

Remember that your fears are in you, and they feel a whole lot scarier trapped in your mind. Let them out. Write them out, visualize yourself overcoming them, draw them, talk about them—just don't keep them trapped inside threatening to throw you off course.

PLAN PART 2: CONNECT PLEASURE AND PAIN

PLEASURE

When I was a kid, I used to make long lists of the things that I wanted in my life. I would write in my diaries forgotten after mere months of diligence about all the reasons I'd live the life of my dreams when I got the chance. I'd imagine what it would feel like to be that girl. It turns out that list-making and daydreaming served me in creating a life I loved, even in elementary school. I had unintentionally focused my mind on what I wanted in my life. I once heard Kerwin Rae say that when he is looking to lock something he wants into his brain, he lists five hundred reasons that reaching that goal, breaking that habit, or learning that skill (you fill in the blank) will be a positive thing in his life.

Five hundred. I'll let you just take that number in for a minute.

He calls it the "Fortune 500 exercise," and while that number is sure to make your eyes bug out of your head, I'd say we can all agree it would give your mind a very clear direction.

Creating a goal may make you feel motivated temporarily. You may eat right for a week or two. You may keep better office hours for a couple of months. You may do a lot of things for a short period of time because motivation is a temporary emotional feeling and will not last.[5] You will need more than motivation to make hard decisions that are ultimately really good for you. You need something that's going to last, and that only happens if you take control of your mind. The Fortune 500 exercise will do just that.

In the Fortune 500 exercise, you're going to connect the thing you want to do (like working out regularly) to something else that you already value. That's the best way to get enough leverage on yourself to make the change you're looking for. You won't do it for something you don't value, so you must tie the action to something you're emotionally connected to.

I can do that by simply asking myself, *What will working out consistently allow me to do?* Here's just a quick list off the top of my head:

1. Working out provides an amazing example to my kids of what it means to take care of themselves.
2. If I work out, I get more high-energy experiences with my family because I'll be more able to run around and sustain the energy it takes to keep up with them.
3. Working out ensures that I'm taking care of my heart. I don't want my daughters to end up with a dead mother at thirty like I did.
4. Taking care of myself makes me happier around my family during the day because I've gotten a lot of my stress and anxiety handled in the gym.
5. Taking care of my body will inspire my kids to want to make themselves physically stronger, which is a great habit for them to develop when they're tweens rather than waiting until they're adults like I did.
6. Time in the gym allows me to know how powerful I really am, which will trickle into the other important areas in my life.
7. Working out with my husband is a great way to connect with him during the day.
8. Working out frees up my mind to think about my spiritual connection to God because I don't have the distraction of screens or obligations.
9. Making my health a priority is nonnegotiable if I want to live long enough to meet my great-grandchildren, and I really want to meet my great-grandchildren.
10. The more I get into the gym, the more confident I am in front of my husband without clothes on.

There are just ten that I was able to write in minutes. I don't want you to write just ten. No, I want you to write five-freaking-hundred of them.

Your brain needs a lot more leverage than that to push you to change. If you're looking for a way to never again be able to talk yourself out of something you know you need to do, the Fortune 500 list is the way.

Ask yourself the question, *What will _____ allow me to do?*

Fill in the blank with the activity or action you find yourself avoiding. Each time you write down and think about a way that one thing connects to something you really value and care about, you're creating *new neural pathways* in your brain. These pathways connect the thing you want to do consistently with the betterment of your life and the lives of the people you love. Those actions now get you closer to your values than taking time away from them. This new neural network will change the way your mind thinks about your goal, and it will go to work on bringing that goal to fruition.

Once you've finished this list and you've made it real in your mind, each time you think about working out, the positive reasons for it will start flooding your brain instead of all the reasons you could get out of it. You'll find you have a lot fewer excuses on the tip of your tongue when you wake up each morning.

The response to this activity will be profound. You can repeat this activity over and over if you're finding yourself unmotivated by something you know is good for you and for your life. This is the secret to motivation. It's not a secret at all. It's a rewiring of your brain.

PAIN

The Dickens Process is something I learned from Tony Robbins on how to make a change that sticks.[6] Named after the author Charles Dickens, the process is about feeling the pain of not taking action so vividly that it no longer becomes an option on the table.

This exercise isn't supposed to feel good. In fact, the point of it is to feel badly enough that you're inspired to change, just like the character Scrooge from Dickens's novel *A Christmas Carol*. Eventually, when visited by the three ghosts, he felt so much pain at the sight of what his future would look like, he changed everything. In an instant, the things he believed he valued in his life became obsolete. He went from being a money-hoarding miser to the happiest, most generous person in town in a single night, no, in an instant. Not by seeing how amazing his life would turn out but by understanding how staying on the path he was on would damage his life and the lives of others in the long run. In the end, he was begging the Ghost of Christmas Yet to Come for a second chance at life to prove he could change it.

This process will work the same for you as it did for Scrooge if you follow these steps:

1. Get completely alone while you do this exercise so you give yourself the opportunity to feel it and verbalize it when you do. You may feel stupid doing this, but the more deeply you get into your mind and into your feelings, the less you'll care what others think. Being alone will give you that judgment-free zone you're looking for.

2. Think about the thing you know you need to change in your life.

Let's imagine that alcohol is becoming a growing concern in your life. You find yourself reaching for a glass of wine earlier and earlier. You sometimes hide your drinking. Often a glass turns into a bottle of wine, and you aren't sure how that happened.

There's no judgment here. None at all. We all have our own harmful-in-the-long-run version of self-protection or numbing we do. It looks different for all of us, and sometimes it's harder to see or feel on others, so we feel alone. You're not alone. So, take that heavy feeling off of you while you explore this.

I want you to imagine that this trend continues down the path of life you're on. In a year from now, how has not making the change you know you need affected your life? How about the people you love? Now let's go five years down the road. What's happening now? What happens in ten years if this little pleasure has turned into an addiction that has you hiding in the closet with a bottle of wine to fill a void or make it through your day? How will that feel? What kinds of things are you missing out on? How is this affecting the things you value so highly right now?

Now I want you to take it to the most extreme consequences for your actions. What will it feel like to find you've created terrible health problems for yourself because of your drinking, and your quality of life diminishes? What happens if your family sits you down and asks you to quit and you find out you can't? How will it feel to drink yourself to death? Imagine your funeral after something like that. How will your kids feel? How might their loss affect them in the future? What did you miss out on because you chose your addiction over experiences?

I want you to really look down the road and the trajectory of your life if you don't make a change right now. Feel what it feels like to see disappointment on the faces of the people you love. Feel what it feels like to be controlled by a substance. Feel it all. Let it land on you. Cry about it. I certainly did. I cried out for mercy when I was thinking of my daughters standing at my funeral feeling disappointed and hurt by my actions toward myself. Don't try to run away from the negative feelings, as we're so prone to do. Don't drown them in something else. Don't numb them. You must feel it all. The more sound you make during this exercise, the more real it will become in your mind.

Your mind doesn't distinguish between an event that you experienced and an event that you make real in your mind. What you set your focus on, your mind will believe. With enough negative leverage, your mind will actively start avoiding the thing it now believes will pull you further away from the things you value. If you get enough negative leverage on yourself, it can be as powerful as the positive, especially if you know it could be the end of you. So make it feel like the end of you.

Linking pleasure and pain to your life is a way that you can control your mind instead of your mind controlling your actions. Your awareness and willingness in this area can make or break your success and ultimately your

> You will not feel fulfilled if you don't have the power to make change in your life. Change is waiting on you.

fulfillment in life. You will not feel fulfilled if you don't have the power to make change in your life. Change is waiting on you. You can use the Fortune 500 exercise and Dickens Process to make change that lasts, in any area of your life.

PLAN PART 3: GO TO WORK

HUNDRED-DAY CHALLENGE

Forty percent of our everyday behavior is habitual.[7] So no wonder so many of us fail to change the habits we know we need to in order to reach our potential. We know we can do hard things, and yet our habits created in childhood are so difficult to break. I read the books; I listened to the talks and the podcasts. I felt like a miserable human when I'd fail the twenty-one-day habit test. *Why is this harder for me than it is for every other person on the internet? What is wrong with me that I can't change this one thing about me?* Ever been there?

Then I got tired of my own bullshit. I got tired of my ego and my mind running the show, and I knew I needed actual strategy. What a powerful day when your ego gets kicked in the teeth by your spirit. That exact moment, for me, is when I decided to take a self-imposed hundred-day challenge.

I'm sure you've seen the hundred-day challenges on social media that pop up to motivate you. Some of them motivate you to try new things. Some of them motivate you creatively. Some are work challenges. Sometimes you'll see physical transformation challenges. All great. I'm especially grateful to Lindsay Jean Thomson for creating her challenge.[8] I initially used her challenge as she intended, to create something every day for one hundred days as a part of a whole project. But then I decided to mold the project into something a little different. Instead of making something new creatively, I decided to make something new internally; I decided I would do this challenge by moving my body.

I didn't want to connect my habit in any way to losing weight. Instead, I focused on goals and benchmarks that would serve me and my values.

My weight should have nothing to do with how I feel about myself. I knew that to be true, and yet my actions weren't following that truth. I was so concerned with how others saw me that I constantly found myself trying to control my weight. It made me unhappy, unfulfilled, and unmotivated, and it made me feel like shit. And I didn't lose weight. Each little step forward would be followed by two steps back. So I wanted to take weight off the table.

And I did.

I walked into my bathroom, I picked up the scale that had witnessed some of my most despicable moments of self-hate, and I threw that shit into the trash. Just like that. I kind of felt like lighting the trash can on fire like you see in the movies, but I didn't want it to be a whole thing with firefighters and insurance and burning the house down. So, I threw it in, and I walked away. Like a boss.

I have no intention of ever knowing my weight again in my entire lifetime. That number is man-made; it means nothing to me. It doesn't measure the things that are meaningful to me. A scale will not help me feel more fulfilled, so it must go. What I really wanted to change in my body wasn't my weight; it was how I felt, it was my overall health and wellness, it was how I saw myself. I needed to seriously dedicate some time in the gym. I needed to pick goals that would help me live the kind of life I feel called to live; and that's one where I am an active participant in keeping my body alive. I wanted to feel stronger, and I wanted to be more flexible. I knew those two focuses would help me meet my highest need at the time: to live a long life. If there is any way that I can impact the number of years that I have here, I want to do that, one step at a time.

For one hundred days I focused on my commitment. I showed up for myself, and each day I reinforced the good habit that I wanted in my brain over the one I didn't want: making excuses and skipping the hard work. I used the chemicals my brain creates for me to make it that much harder to quit the next day. I didn't obsess over what I looked like in the gym. I destroyed my ego around what I wanted people to think about me by posting videos of my workouts, which, let's be honest, aren't flattering. But they are real, and they show the changes that I was able to make in one hundred days. And I no longer have any opinions about what people should think about my gym time. I stopped trying to control that. Actually, I started realizing I never actually could. I got very realistic about the changes I wanted to make, and I walked away from those one hundred days much stronger and much more flexible.

I lost a ton of weight, but that's just a cherry on top for me as I continue to focus on things I can control. I got pretty good at yoga in that short amount of time just because I was consistent with my time and effort in the gym. I no longer wanted the shortcut because I knew it wouldn't lead me to my goals. I wanted the hard way. I wanted it to burn. I wanted to feel it. And each drop of sweat became one step closer to a long and healthy life.

When those one hundred days were up, it wasn't a hard decision to go for the second round right away. And two hundred became three hundred. This year I will have worked out every day for 365 days. And I've done it for no other reason than to prove to myself that I can. If I can do this every day for a year, there is nothing I can't do. I know what pain feels like. I understand what dedication takes. I can do hard things. My mind has no leverage on me like it used to. There is no "You're not fill-in-the-blank enough anymore" because I know I am enough to desire hard changes in my life, and I will become the person who is mentally and physically ready for anything put before me.

The 100-Day Challenge has had a profound impact on the way I live all six cornerstones of a good life.

LOVE
YOURSELF
THROUGH THE PROCESS

INSTEAD OF HATING YOURSELF
THROUGH IT

PART 2

THE SIX CORNERSTONES OF A GOOD LIFE

You ready to start applying what you're learning to your life? This is the part where this book will come alive for you. This is the part I'm most excited for you to learn. I'm going to unpack the process in each area so you're guided through the shift. I'm going to give you step-by-step instructions for each of the six cornerstones.

This is what's about to go down in this section of the book:
- You're going to go one by one through each cornerstone.
- You're going to be challenged to think differently and make changes and find true fulfillment in each one.
- We're going to walk through the WOOP experience for each cornerstone. I'll give you some examples of what fulfillment might look like and some insights that make each section as easy as possible for follow-through.

One thing I want to encourage you to do is to see yourself with a lot of grace. When I say grace, I mean love even when you feel you don't deserve it. Love yourself through this process instead of hating yourself through it. Remember, without every decision you've ever made, you wouldn't be right here, reading this book, about to make a plan for the rest of it. You need the mistakes. You need the lessons.

Step into part 2 of this book as the person you have the potential to be.

The self-loathing, complaining, and negativity become the evidence our mind needs to keep us safe and small at home. At some point, you're going to have to tell that mindset to get the hell out of your house. If you want to build a life you love, you cannot believe you deserve it easily and you cannot run away from the fight to get it. It's going to be a challenge, but I'm going to be here to guide you through it.

When I decided to go all in on the idea of a "good life," I didn't fully believe it was possible for me. But that was because I was going about the process all wrong. I naively believed that in order for me to build this kind of life, I'd have to do it all and I'd have to do it all at one time. Because my mind knows that's the best way to get me to stay small, it gives me a perfect excuse to not even try.

> **As soon as you shift your mindset around challenges, everything changes.**

As soon as you shift your mindset around challenges, everything changes. You can have it all, but you can't do it all at one time. Here are some tips before we take this next fulfilling step together . . .

READINESS TIPS

1. If you're the praying, meditating, or journaling type, I highly recommend it through this process.
2. Take note of how you feel and what is coming to you.
3. Sit in any discomfort without numbing. Pro tip: no screens, no Wi-Fi.

4. Celebrate every good feeling with all of the enthusiasm in your body. Dance. Jump. Scream. Play loud music. Smile. Laugh. Move your body. Make noise. The more enthusiastic you are, the more your mind will take in what you're doing here and find a way to make it happen.

I'm proud of you. You've made it through the first phase, and now you've got all you need for the next. I get it if you're feeling a little anxious, but know that I've got your back and you've got this. Collect these tools, and let's get to our set appointment with the six cornerstones of a good life. This is going to be the best kind of work.

YOU CAN HAVE IT ALL

BUT YOU CAN'T DO IT ALL AT ONCE

PERSONAL FULFILLMENT

We're starting with personal fulfillment because it's the one cornerstone of the six that we'll all push to the back burner if given the chance to focus elsewhere. There's a misconception that it's selfish to think or act in our own interest. I think it's the words "our own interest" that trip us up. What if I said acting in the interest of yourself is your responsibility? You alone are responsible for your life and the decisions you make.

Culturally, we're conditioned to believe we are to act in the best interest of the greater good. The problem is that we all disagree on what the greater good is. Don't believe me? Think back to the fighting over masks, vaccines, quarantine orders, and riots from 2020. We wouldn't want others to think us selfish, so we just go along to get along. We make decisions about our time, money, and desires based on what will be acceptable to the people who have voices in our lives. Sometimes those voices are those of strangers and we give them weight. This is one time where I want you to think only of you. This series of activities is about you. It's not about your kids; that's in relationships. It's not about what you should be doing. This section isn't about anything but your responsibility to find personal fulfillment.

First, let's define what I mean by personal fulfillment. Personal fulfillment in this context is simply your ability to realize your deepest desires and capacities. It may feel like waking up excited to go experience something new, like your first day of school as a kid. Remember how easy it was to get up on the first day of school when we were little? It may also feel like going to bed knowing you did your best to make yourself more capable and competent for the following day, like on the days you finally tackle that one item on your to-do list that you had been procrastinating on. It might feel like experiencing something you've waited for all of your life. That's how I feel when I travel and explore.

I'll tell you what it won't feel like: an obligation. Your personal fulfillment isn't about other people. It's not about the things others want to do with you. It's not about what others need from you. It's not about someone else's goals. I believe what will fulfill you personally is between you and your creator. The desires of your spirit and your purpose will feel like an intimate dance with the divine. You will probably be tired as you're dancing. It may even be confusing or hard to follow the steps. You may mess up a few times as you learn how to move around the dance floor. Make no mistake; you are the main event. The floor is yours, and it will feel like you're in the right place. Everyone else in your life are the spectators, and the good ones will be there clapping for you when you take your bow. Take up every square inch of that dance floor, my friends. Dance with all the enthusiasm you can muster because we need your example.

> The desires of your spirit and your purpose will feel like an intimate dance with the divine.

How many times have you sacrificed the thing you wanted for what others wanted? How many times have you failed to say what you want because you're afraid of what others may think of you? How many times have you bent over backward for others but refused to do the same or expect the same for yourself?

My friend Andrea is perhaps the boldest person I know when it comes to her personal fulfillment. This woman is an absolute beast. She is strong, beautiful, put-together, smart, funny, intuitive, understanding, and an extremely hard worker. A couple of years ago, she up and left her six-figure job at a billion-dollar corporation to chase her own personal fulfillment.

Andrea had a job she loved, but it was running her into the ground. She couldn't even spend the money she was making because she didn't have time. She didn't have the relationships she wanted in her life; she didn't have the personal fulfillment; she wasn't living the life of her dreams. One day, while walking her dog after another eighteen-hour day at work, she asked herself if how she was spending all of her days was fulfilling her. Andrea knew instantly that she had to leave her job in order to get a hold of the other five cornerstones of a good life. She had to walk away from a good thing for a better thing. She had to burn her old life to the ground.

So she did.

She quit her job and she took the money she had saved, her possessions, and her dog, and she moved to a studio apartment on the beach in California. She took the time to connect with her spirit by being quiet, walking the beach, meditating, and journaling. She traveled the world alone. She sat in cafés and bars in foreign cities without a plan. She began taking care of her body and her mind. She lived simply and efficiently, focused only on what she needed to fulfill herself. Andrea made Andrea her only focus for the first time in maybe ever. During that time when she was refinding herself, I barely talked to her. She wasn't posting her adventures all over social media; she wasn't calling to check in. She didn't have time for any of that.

She was busy finding Andrea again. She woke up to reality.

And when we did connect, she had a new relationship in her life; she was taking care of herself; she was preparing to reenter the workforce with the proper boundaries around what's sacred to her. There was a joy in her voice on the phone that day that was the real Andrea. She's a magnet for the things she wants in life because she was willing to burn the old one to the ground in search of something new and more aligned to her purpose.

That's a big risk to take, which is why I chose to share Andrea's story. Leaving a job you're golden-handcuffed to for total and complete uncertainty? What kind of crazed lunatic does that? I hope the answer will be all of us. Our fulfillment is worth discovering what's on the other side of normal.

> **Our fulfillment is worth discovering what's on the other side of normal.**

I think this self-fulfillment problem has less to do with selflessness and more to do with conditioning, fear, and issues of self-worth. Our brains are goal-seeking by nature. Remember that whatever we put into our subconscious mind, it will go to work to achieve. For your betterment or the opposite, if you say it and concentrate on it, your mind will find it. That's why I believe that people who get caught up in their fear end up summoning it right to their front door. As I mentioned earlier, what you fear, you draw near. But there is nothing to fear. Everything on this planet is working in your favor, even the hard stuff. So those who set their minds to improving the lives of everyone else but themselves will get just that. And that everyone-else-is-happy-but-me-so-I'll-just-pretend feeling gets old and turns to resentment really fast.

Your personal wants, desires, and needs for yourself are important. They're important for you and they're important for the people who know and love you, including your family and your friends. You'll be more capable of being fully present with others if you're fulfilled in your personal life by taking care of you. You'll be a better example to your family if you make yourself a priority because you will want them to make themselves a priority someday. How will they learn that if not from you? You'll be ready to help where you're needed and give when you're needed if your cup is full. That only happens when you make time to do the things that you want.

Your personal goals can be absolutely all over the map. They can be hard things you want to learn or places you want to visit. Your personal desires can be hobby related or they can be as simple as taking time each day to read or sit in a hot bath simply because it brings you joy.

The other five cornerstones of a good life are not where your personal dreams go to die. No one thing is more important than the other. In fact, I've learned that one without the others just isn't the whole picture of a good life. It's not that your life won't be considered "good" if you only nail a few areas, but you'll always feel like something is missing.

When I was kicking ass and taking names at work and making what I considered to be "Scrooge McDuck money" to go along with it, I was happy. I was also keenly aware that if I didn't decide to try to stay alive at some point in my life by taking care of my health and connecting with my creator, I wouldn't be able to enjoy it for long. I knew in my heart and soul that something was missing, and it wasn't hard to pinpoint exactly what it was that I needed in my life.

Writing personal goals is some of the most fun I can have by myself. I know, I'm a party animal, but stick with me here. Imagining how my life will change when I see parts of the world I'm craving, or thinking about how it will feel to master a skill I've had my eye on, is really satisfying. It feels good. You should try it.

In 2008, when Michael and I were super poor with newborn twins at home, we watched the Super Bowl on TV one February evening. We laughed over how we wished we were there. "Wouldn't it be cool to go to the Super Bowl? I want to do that one day." As huge fans of the game, we just wanted to experience the energy and excitement of the biggest game of the year.

That day we looked at each other directly in the eyes with a huge smile on our faces and we agreed that if we ever made a million dollars in a year, we'd take a part of that money and we'd go to the Super Bowl no matter who was playing. I'm not sure if I really believed it. The Super Bowl when you can barely rub two pennies together feels like planning a trip to Mars with Elon. My decision to start a business led to my husband quitting his job and helping me start eight others in the women's entrepreneurship space. Fast-forward seven long, hard, and full years: Michael and I walked into the stadium in Glendale, Arizona, to watch the Seattle Seahawks take on the New England Patriots in Super Bowl 49. We sat in our seats on the fifty-yard line, and we looked at each other directly in the eyes with huge smiles on our faces and said, "I can't believe we are here."

We did it. We both made a dream experience happen. It was never about the money. It was never about what other people thought of our goal. It was always about an experience that most people only dream of. Sitting in a place that I was sure I'd never be able to was as shocking as it was exciting. Since then, Michael and I have made it back to the Super Bowl every year to celebrate our work success. I'm so grateful that desire was put inside of us. It's been quite an experience each year, and we take the time to really connect with one another and celebrate each other.

Believe me, what you tell your mind, it will go to work to make it happen. The day we said the plan out loud was the day my mind went to work on sitting in those seats at a Super Bowl someday in the future, and Michael's did the same. Some people would never dream of spending the time and money on such a "frivolous" thrill in their lives. That's okay because this one's mine. Your goals for yourself aren't about other people.

> **Believe me, what you tell your mind, it will go to work to make it happen.**

The great news about this whole personal business is that it's exactly that, personal! This isn't about anyone else and it's not for anyone else. Personal fulfillment is strictly for you. It's not that you have to do them alone, it's that they're not written to please anyone else. That includes your kids, and it includes your spouse. Doing things with them is one thing; doing things for them is completely another.

Here are some ideas to spark your imagination and perhaps remind you of ways you can fill your personal fulfillment cup. I'm going to ask a series of questions. Feel free to highlight the ones that may connect to you on a personal level so that you know where to begin when it comes to actually planning your time and goals.

- What kinds of things do you like to do with your time?
- What do you want people to say you were skilled at?
- What have you always dreamed of trying?
- What is one thing you think might be fun but is super scary for you?
- What kinds of things would you like to learn about your family or your ancestry?
- Where would you like to travel to with your group of friends?
- Where would you want to go on a trip with just your spouse?
- What kinds of places around the world would you want to experience with your family (kids or extended family)?
- What kind of hobby do you wish you had?
- Do you have the desire to learn a new language?
- What kinds of things would you want to learn if you were able to find a mentor?
- What kinds of personal goals have you put off because you just don't have the time?
- If you could, what kind of nonprofit would you start to help a cause close to your heart?
- Would journaling be a good way for you to take some time for yourself?
- Who would you send handwritten notes to, telling them how they've helped you or how grateful you are for them?
- What would you make if you suddenly knew how and you could give it away to someone?
- Have you dreamed of cutting down on clutter around your house and in your life?

- What kinds of events would you want tickets to if money were no object?
- If you had to spend a month away from your house, where would you go within the country you already live in? How about abroad?
- What kinds of concerts would you want to go to?
- If you had all the time in the world, what kind of legacy or lesson would you want to leave for your kids?
- How many of the natural wonders of the world would you want to see? How about national parks?
- What kinds of things could you do every day that would make an impact on your mental health?
- What kind of car do you want to drive?
- Where do you want to live?
- If you could redecorate a room in your house, what style would you do it in?
- Are there any influential people in your life you've never met that you'd like to?

Y'all, this is not a complete list. You don't have to want to do any of that for yourself in your life. But you do have to want to do something. You're reading this book right now because you know there's another level in you and you want more fulfillment and joy in your life. We can all say that. Let's not keep ourselves stuck constantly thinking about other people and neglecting our own desires, no matter how big or how small.

Before we go all morbid around here, let's get real. If you're sixty years old and you have no savings account, you're going to have to get really creative about the amount of time, energy, and money you'll need for each thing you want. I'm not saying there's no way to achieve absolutely anything at any age (again, remember Joan); I'm saying that for some it's going to be more difficult and therefore the level of dedication will have to be higher.

- Be realistic about the things you can achieve along with the commitments and realities you have to contend with for your free time.

- Make a priority list of the things you want to achieve in your personal life, and run after the things that are actually going to bring you a good return on your investment for your time.

I'm looking at you, parents.

We know that when kids are little, your time is cut short because it's a full-time job just to, you know, keep them alive. Making yourself a priority in the day is going to be difficult on some days, and it's going to take support from your community (spouse, family, friends, and so on) to get it done. Most importantly, it's going to take laser-like focus from you in order to get it down if your time is pulled in a lot of directions. Find ways to fit your personal fulfillment into your day by doing a kid switch with a friend or neighbor for some free time to work on what you need. Instead of spending nap times cleaning up the house or doing chores, take some of that time for you and what you want. When I was working really hard on my personal fulfillment, I asked my husband for time. I asked him to pitch in extra here and there. I asked for what I needed, which seems like a novel concept but shouldn't be. Communicate what you need, and you'll be surprised how fast you get it.

And here's another truth for the parents or the extremely busy: this may not be the season where you go all in on your personal fulfillment, but that doesn't mean you don't think about it at all. At one point, you will be forced to make yourself a priority for your own fulfillment. Don't put yourself last, because personal fulfillment has been one of my greatest joys. Doing things just for the pure joy of doing them and because I like them is so freaking fun. We had personal fulfillment down when we were kids, didn't we? And somehow we lost it as we grew up and became obsessed with busy and forgot why we're here.

Let's put your personal goals and desires through the WOOP experience.

WISH

CONTEMPLATE YOUR DEATH

If you were to die today, what kinds of things would you have missed out on that you've always wanted to do but never made a priority? If you're looking at your family and friends, what are they saying about you? Are they telling stories about how you had the guts to follow your fulfillment? How about your kids? What kind of example have you set for them about how important their personal desires are? What do you wish you would have done more of in your life?

DESIRE CHANGE

Do you want to change this? I'm asking honestly because I think so many women will push personal fulfillment off of their priority lists because it goes against our societal conditioning that says, "What kind of woman chooses to do something for herself when her kids need her?" So ask yourself, and answer honestly: Do you have a desire to become personally fulfilled? If you don't, could it be that now isn't the right time? Is it because you're fearful? Could it be because you were conditioned to be "selfless"? I challenge you to lean into the reason you may resist right now.

Listen, I didn't put my personal fulfillment first when I decided I wanted to go to the Super Bowl. That didn't become a reality for seven years. I was knee-deep in my business and financial fulfillment at that time, but it came anyway because I was brave enough to say it when it felt impossible. I never, ever, ever worked for that experience. It was just in my mind as something we would do one day. And the day came for me rather than the other way around.

> Priorities are good, but dreaming never hurts!

You can do this, even if your personal fulfillment isn't the highest on your priority list. Priorities are good, but dreaming never hurts!

OUTCOME

THINK FROM A SPIRITUAL PERSPECTIVE

What is your spirit leading you toward? A new hobby? A new way to discover the things you love? Time alone to just sit and get to know yourself again? What can you do to connect to your spirit so you can learn the truth about who you are and what you're capable of? What do you need to do to love yourself more? Your spirit is begging you to make yourself a priority.

CONNECT WITH YOUR VALUES

Go back to that values list and discover what you might be missing personally.

If you love variety in your life but you find yourself doing the same thing over and over again, as I did when my kids were little, how can you stay true to your value of variety and still be consistent for your kids? I did that through hobbies when my kids were young. I would get my camera out and take photos as we traveled or were out in the day. I documented our lives through scrapbooking and using my hands to create something.

What can you do right now to connect your need to make yourself a priority to one of the values that's already on the list? As someone who had a difficult time making herself a priority, I'm begging you to do it. I can only be as good for others as I am for myself. Show up for yourself in a way that honors your values and the things that are important in your life. You should absolutely be one of those things.

OBSTACLE

Let's take some time to list out the obstacles we may find along the path to personal fulfillment. For Andrea, the obstacles were self-limiting. Everything that she perceived as an obstacle to her personal fulfillment was self-imposed. If she left her job, would she have enough money to survive? Would she find another job? Personal obstacles are often more about limiting beliefs than they are about something physically standing in the way of you feeling fulfilled in your personal life. As you list your obstacles, you may be tempted to feel overwhelmed by the things standing in your way. Remember that every obstacle, problem, or roadblock in our path is working for us. These hard days, which you will have, are preparing you for something so much greater down the road.

Take some time to journal in a stream-of-consciousness style or in list style what might pop up as you pursue making yourself and the things that you're interested in a priority.

- What kinds of things might hold you back from the significance you're seeking personally?
- How will others react when you start doing things for yourself?
- How might your new focus throw off the balance in some other areas?
- Are there conversations you need to have?
- Are there plans you need to make in advance to ensure you have the ability to focus on you? Do you need to get out of your own way and just do the thing, take the class, or travel there?
- Is your packed schedule a problem for your personal fulfillment?

PLAN

DETERMINE YOUR ACTION PLAN

Make a list of at least ten actions that you can take in the next month to start prioritizing yourself and the things you want for your life. You don't have to do all of them. For now, you're just writing down ideas so you can turn back to them for a quick list of action items when you need them. If you're having a hard time coming up with what that might look like, perhaps you should write it out, do a visualization meditation, or even draw where you're at now and where you want to be in the future. But then you need to ask yourself the question about what three things you need to do right now to make your future a reality. The action is required for success.

CONNECT PLEASURE AND PAIN

This Fortune 500 list is going to be fun because it's going to force you to connect the things you want to all the ways it's going to help others or put you in the other five cornerstones. This is the part where you list five hundred benefits to you finding personal fulfillment in your life. Enough benefit and you'll never want to quit. You're going to write down all the ways that your personal fulfillment will positively affect your marriage, your relationships, your business, your health, and your finances. Listing five hundred is hard work; it's going to take time, but if you can find five hundred benefits to you making a change, the likelihood that it sticks is much higher.

If you're stuck, don't avoid the Dickens Process, in which you'll go inside your mind's eye and imagine what the future will be like if you never make a change. What will your life look like at the end if you never find personal fulfillment? What example will you be for the people who love you and look up to you, like kids or family and friends? I had to do that for myself in order to take action for me because it just didn't seem natural. I knew it was something I wanted to do but not something I thought I needed to do. I was wrong. You need to think about and focus on your personal fulfillment aside from every other part of your life. And if it takes the worst situation imaginable to get you to do that, so be it!

GO TO WORK

The original hundred-day challenge was a personal challenge; I wanted to work out every day for one hundred days, not because I wanted to lose weight but because I wanted to stick to something that was purely for me. I wanted to see what that kind of activity would do to my mindset. I wanted to prove to myself that I was a badass. What kind of little activity can you dedicate your time to every day for one hundred days to help you form a new habit? How can this little activity spark joy and excitement in you despite the fact that you have to sacrifice for it? Don't put yourself last. Don't put this challenge off so long that you forget who you are and what lights you up inside. Go do things just for you for one hundred days straight and see how it changes you and challenges you.

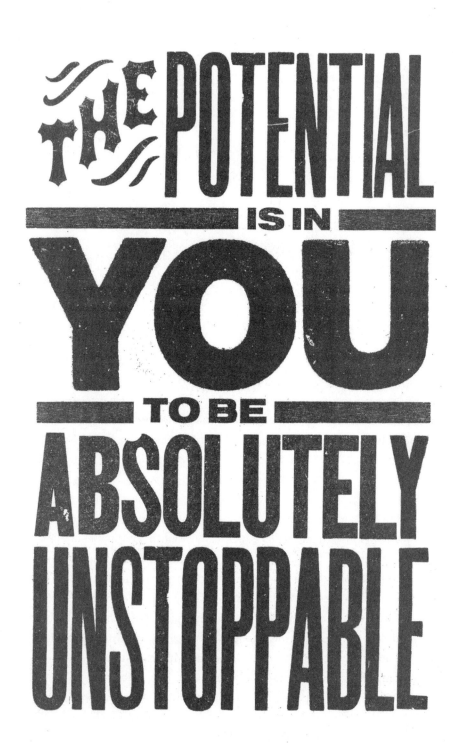

WORK/BUSINESS FULFILLMENT

Squeee! I really love to talk about work and business. Chances are you probably know me through that. We probably connected and bonded over how to build a thriving business. My business has been a source of great pride, love, and fulfillment for me personally. Everything I did for work in the last decade was to support entrepreneurs. I speak, write, create workshops, and find ways to meet needs for my target market by filling holes in the industry. For example, I own a stock photography site where I produce high-quality, unique, and beautiful images for entrepreneurs who don't know how to shoot or don't have the time for it. My goal is to make advertising easier and to help entrepreneurs stand out with eye-catching images. My business allows me to have something that I own to create any number of options for myself. My business helps me feel fulfilled in my personal life, finances, relationships, and work and has led me down the path to a spiritual awakening. My business was the catalyst for my strong desire for more in my life.

I'm a huge proponent of entrepreneurship, especially for women, because I think there are so many lessons in owning your own business that affect more than just your work. My business has affected absolutely every part of my life, from being a more patient mom after dealing with adults all day to becoming a healthier version of me by discovering I need strong boundaries. I realize that entrepreneurship isn't going to be what every person wants. I'm not going to try to push you in any direction if you have your mind made up. If you think entrepreneurship might be for you, I want to emphasize how important that may be to your story. Owning a business of your own will offer up opportunities for you to fail and win. It will destroy your ego, which is good for all of us. It will keep you up at night fighting for the life of your business and your vision for it. And you'll do it all happily because your business means something to you and you value it.

If you're a stay-at-home parent, you absolutely can and should consider that to be part of your work in that season of your life. You're raising humans. Like real ones. When my twins were newborns, I was a complete and total disaster to be around. I would have had a really hard time keeping up with my business at that time. Once they got older, the pull toward entrepreneurship continued to tug at me. If that's the case for you, don't be afraid to show your kids what a parent can do, even with kids at home. I love that my kids have seen me work. My mom took great pride in staying home with us when we were in our early years before she entered into entrepreneurship. I am so grateful to have been able to stay at home with my kids while I built a business.

There's no wrong way to fulfill this part of you. You can do that as a parent staying at home, at a corporate job, volunteering at a nonprofit, or by starting a business of your own. No one way is right or wrong. The options are there for you to work through with your spirit. I believe a big part of our fulfillment is working toward something that we care about. I find that my work does that for me. I care about female entrepreneurs. I care about women who are staying home with their kids and have the guts to pursue a business at the same time. I care about their health, wealth, and happiness. So it's not hard for me to pour my time and effort into making that a priority in my life. At one point, it became so important to me that it was almost all I thought about. I began to systematically cut the attention I gave to the other parts of my life so I had more time to grow my business.

When I was building my first big business, which was in the natural health and wellness space, I put 100 percent of my effort into the success of it knowing I would be spending some of the time, energy, and resources on work that I would normally dedicate to other areas. My work goal directly correlated to my personal goals and my financial goals. I was laser focused on my financial goals with the understanding that some of the goals for the other values correlated and the ones that didn't, I could and would build soon after. This looked like me committing to one family breakfast a week. We went to breakfast every Saturday as a family, no excuses, no exceptions. Outside of this commitment to my family, I worked the majority of the time. I worked seven days a week and averaged around one hundred hours a week, all while staying home with my kids. This decision was transformative for our family.

It was insane and it was perfect at the same time. There's a lie out there that you can't do both. Yes, you can. You just have to decide to be okay with imperfect. Sometimes you'll work in the car while your kids are at practice. Sometimes you'll throw goldfish crackers down the hall one hundred times to keep them occupied while you respond to customers or put some time in. You work during nap times, you find a babysitter to help during the week, you teach your kids to be self-sufficient, and you give up control of what it will look like. There can be no attachment to the result; I promise you, it's going to look and feel differently than you think. Attaching to the result closes you off to the possibility that the result is something you never thought of. Attaching to a result leads to frustration and unmet expectations.

My house was in a state of emergency. My kids had to ask me for snacks at least five times before I could drag myself away from my office to get them. My friends never heard from me. My husband and I didn't connect every day the way we do now. My bank account showed more money than ever before, but I didn't have any time to spend it. My health declined rapidly from stress and overwork. I ignored my body and pushed myself really hard for a couple of years. It was hard, and that may not work for some families, but it was worth it for us. Even when I was exhausted and knew I could be using my time for something else that would be more acceptable for a young mom, I was happy. I was fulfilled by my work, and I'm proud that I've shown my daughters from an early age to make their dreams a priority.

But that time came with a cutoff date. Before I started, I sat down with Michael, and we agreed that I'd work as hard as I could to get my business off the ground for two years. And if after that time it wasn't working for him, then it wasn't working for me, and I'd walk away. My marriage is more important than my business because I value it higher. I was willing to make sure that the business worked for both of us. And we stuck to that plan. Instead of telling me to quit my work after those two years were up, Michael told me I needed a counselor. And I did. I was completely addicted to my work. I love it. It was as easy to become addicted to as Texas Sheet Cake—you know the one with the icing on top that gets a little crispy on the outside but is soft and yummy on the inside? Yeah, my business feels like that to me. Full-scale, five-alarm addiction.

And I worked through that. My ability to compartmentalize my life and my goals is the reason that I can now afford to focus on the other areas. I've been able to retire from one of my businesses and sell a few others. The work is my passion and my calling, but it's also a means to an end. My work is something that I love and it's something that I needed at that time to be able to dream bigger about what my life could hold for me and my family.

I no longer do one-hundred-hour workweeks. I no longer even work full-time. That may change in the future if a new idea comes to me, but I no longer need to focus all of my time, attention, and effort on a business. I already did that part. The foundation has been laid and now I get to go use the free time that I've earned to affect other parts of my life.

Remember what we talked about—balance is an illusion. It's Harry

Houdini-type magic. I can't stress that enough. You can't do it all, so don't try to. Let the parts of your life that aren't high on the priority list stand idle for a little while as you focus your attention on what you need. Things like dishes put away and laundry folded and showers every day can wait if you need them to. If what you need is money, perhaps a business is a good place to start. Maybe go look for another job that gives you more flexibility and allows you more time to do the things that are a high priority for you. I repeat: you don't have to do it all. Choose what to set aside. When you do this, you're not letting balls drop. You are intentionally putting them down. Communicate your plan so that other people don't feel neglected and then go out and do what you need to do to live a life of fulfillment and purpose. Don't worry about what others have to say about how you accomplish your goals.

Do it in the way that works best for you.

On the other side of that coin, I would be remiss if I didn't talk to you about what to do if you find yourself a workaholic like I did in my career. I became so addicted to my work I didn't know how to stop. If it's time for you to take a break from work for a time or to shift directions, do it.

> You're not letting balls drop. You are intentionally putting them down.

Communicate clearly what you want. If my mom had taken some time to step back from work for a bit and not let her money concerns bleed into how much time she spent working, she may have been able to save herself from her early heart attack. Destroying your health long-term isn't worth your job. *Ever.* *steps off soapbox*

NO MORE TORTURE

A lot of people think their work needs to feel like a punishment in order for them to "earn" the position or deserve the pay. A lot of people believe that if they just keep grinding even though they hate what they're doing, they'll get rich eventually.

Fundamentally, both of those beliefs are wrong.

If you hate it, that's your sign that you're not in the correct place to fulfill your life's purpose. You will not hate your purpose. You'll never be rich doing something you dread because rich is a state of mind that you will achieve when you find meaningful work that you love doing. A rich work life rarely has anything to do with money.

Stop torturing yourself and saying yes to shit you hate. It's not serving you, and you're not here to fulfill someone else's purpose. All of these noes you're about to say will become the platform that the life you love will be built on. It won't be easy. You'll definitely catch hell from the people who are used to you putting yourself last—people who take advantage of your lack of boundaries or people whom you constantly find yourself rescuing. You'll feel bad about it at first. And then you'll remember you aren't a secondary character in someone else's story. You're the lead in your own story, and it's up to you to tell it.

You're the lead in your own story, and it's up to you to tell it.

If you feel like you have a business way down deep inside of you, I hope you will pursue that calling. We need more entrepreneurs and small businesses. Our world needs us. I need you. My girls need you. Your family needs you. My book *Boss Up!* was written with you in mind. I highly recommend that you check it out when you're making plans for action in the WOOP experience. It will walk you through starting and building a business that fulfills you in much more detail than this chapter.

Whatever desire for work is in you, I hope you believe the potential is in you to be absolutely unstoppable. Set big dreams for yourself and see who you discover under all that work and all those challenges. My work has made me resilient, focused, and prepared for anything that life might want to throw at me. I hope you'll feel the same about the work you do every day.

Let's WOOP experience this sucker:

WISH

CONTEMPLATE YOUR DEATH

If today was your last day on earth, would you regret anything about the time you spent working in your life? Many people say they wish they had spent more time with family and less time focused on work. Is that true for you? If so, is there a way you could combine your family and work time? Is there a way you can focus on one to free you up for the other in the coming years or months? Will you wish you had made the career move that you always felt in your gut was right for you, or will you regret letting fear keep you in one place? Will you wish you'd quit that job? Started that company? Switched to an industry you loved and out of one you hated?

DESIRE CHANGE

How many years do you have left to work before retirement? Is it enough time at your current salary or income to sustain the way you live your life or fund the way you want to live your life? Are there changes you can make right now that feel scary to you that may allow you to live in a completely different way? Are you content in your work right now, or do you feel the draw to something else? Is there a desire in you to make some changes around how, where, and when you work? If the desire for change is there, it's time to admit that there's another level in you somewhere.

OUTCOME

THINK FROM A SPIRITUAL PERSPECTIVE

What do you want when you think nobody is paying attention? Do you find yourself afraid to take risks when it comes to work? How could you spend part of your time bringing in an income and being fulfilled by meaningful work at the same time? Is there anything that God has revealed to you that you've been ignoring when it comes to work? Is the work you do working for the rest of your family and the things you value?

CONNECT WITH YOUR VALUES

How can you connect the work that you do or desire to do to your core values that are already meaningful for you? Whenever I find myself procrastinating on work or putting it off, I try to connect the work I'm doing on that day to something I really value. For example, adventure and exploring are high values for me. I need to see the world. I need to connect to the earth and God's creation. I need to connect with other cultures. Those are things I value way down deep. I cannot possibly do the things I want to in my life as far as travel is concerned if I don't have any money. My business brings me the money to go do the things I love. So, I connect the work I'm doing right now to a trip in the future or a plan for something new. I connect the work I'm doing today to the safety net I want to build for my family. I connect the work I'm doing today to the values and goals I have in the other parts of my life. That makes it a lot easier to get into the office and put in a full day of work with a good attitude.

OBSTACLE

What kinds of things stand in the way of the kind of work you want to do? I want you to take some time to journal about this. You can write in a stream of consciousness, or you can make lists. The point of this exercise is to be aware so when you make a plan to push forward, you're prepared for the obstacles that will surely be thrown your way.

I often have people come to me with questions on how they can leave the job they're in or create a new business when they're golden-handcuffed to a job that sucks the life out of them. Time and money pressures are so real and so difficult to get out of if you never make a plan for it. Being golden-handcuffed is a situation where you take a job that pays you so much for your time that you will have a hard time ever leaving them because finding an equal-paying job elsewhere feels impossible. Instead of staying stuck, make a plan to cut your expenses by 10 percent, 20 percent, or 25 percent so that you can focus on some work fulfillment in an environment that may not pay as much right now but offers more flexibility. There's always a way around an obstacle, and sometimes it might be just ripping off the Band-Aid, quitting your job, and trusting that you'll make something new happen. Obstacles aren't meant to stop you; they're meant to wake you up to being more capable and competent.

> Obstacles aren't meant to stop you; they're meant to wake you up to being more capable and competent.

Will your family have an issue with you wanting to work if you don't now?

Will you have support from your family and friends if you decide to start a new business or take a new job?

Will the work you do stimulate and excite you while also bringing in enough money to pay the bills and pursue a life of significance?

How might you find yourself being the biggest roadblock to your work success in the future?

Are there things you need to deal with now so that they don't become bigger issues if you find yourself spending a lot of time and energy at work?

What is taking the most time away from work that you may have to set aside to accomplish your work goals?

PLAN

DETERMINE YOUR ACTION PLAN

What do you need to do at work to allow you to pursue the other parts of your life in the future? What three things can you do this week to get your plan off the ground and put some intention into your actions?

Who do you know who can help you?

How can you enlist help?

How can you incorporate your family into your plan for success and fulfillment at work? Or do you even need to do that?

Your work is one thing that can be completely for you if you want it to. Don't make the mistake of believing your work is only for others. It's not. Your happiness and fulfillment are the point of this exercise.

CONNECT PLEASURE AND PAIN

I have found the Fortune 500 exercise to be something so good for people who feel stuck in their job. If you're struggling to feel fulfillment at work, change is an option, but changing your mindset is also an option. Take all the time you need to make a list of the five hundred reasons that working on your business, going to work, or building something new to work on is going to affect your life positively. How will it affect the other five cornerstones of a good life for you? If you need more motivation or you're specifically struggling with your attitude and love for work, the Dickens Process might be a great tool for you to use to change your mindset.

GO TO WORK

What will you do for your hundred-day challenge at work? It could be as easy as setting aside thirty distraction-free minutes to work on your to-do list every day. Maybe it's tackling something you put off every day. Maybe you get some coworkers to do the hundred-day challenge with you to push yourself beyond your threshold for success.

BE
DONE
BEING BROKE

SAY TO YOURSELF
I'LL NEVER
DO THAT AGAIN

FINANCIAL FULFILLMENT

So there I was putting a $7.02 pack of chicken back and grabbing one that was $6.93 instead . . . Oh, don't act like you've never done that! Finances. Insert cry-face emoji, right?

Money is hard to talk about, hard to think about, and really hard to keep sometimes, right? The more you talk about money and increase your financial vocabulary, the easier it will become to normalize it in your life and your everyday intentions. I believe the biggest financial obstacle you'll face is your mindset. Mindset has destroyed more wealth than the economy ever could. Money and finances are a challenge for most of us.

> **Mindset has destroyed more wealth than the economy ever could.**

Michael and I recently sat down with our attorney to go over our will and trust. We worked out all the details about what was to go where and how our kids will be taken care of should Michael and I not be able to do the job. And as we started to do the math, we realized just how well we had prepared to "take care" of our kids in the event of our deaths. I started to get nervous about handing over checks to kids who haven't earned the financial success. What could that do to them? I've seen a lot of trust-fund kids destroy their lives with that money. How could I keep that from being my kids? I don't know anything about this stuff because this is not the situation I grew up in. I'm a first-generation and self-made millionaire. This is completely foreign to me.

And the answer came in a session with my counselor where he said, "It's not the money that will hurt them, it's the mindset." And here's what he meant.

Anyone who receives anything, from money, or a relationship, to something as small as a compliment, will set their minds on destroying that good thing if they feel undeserving. Classic self-sabotage. They don't have to try. They don't have to think about it. Most likely they won't think about it. They'll simply create a story about that money and their mind will go to work to make their beliefs reality. But the difference between many rich kids who made their money and many rich kids who were given the money is simply a mindset.

Here's what I know: if something does happen to us and my kids absolutely blow the money or assets they get in their trust, that's their challenge to overcome. It's going to be a lesson they need to learn.

What Michael and I really need to be focusing on right now is the mindset of our daughters while they're young and still living under our roof. We need to teach them that they aren't entitled to anything—absolutely nothing. Nothing is guaranteed and nothing is promised, but remember our twelve laws, specifically the law of compensation: you'll get exactly the thing you deserve, nothing more and nothing less. It's up to us to teach them to accept the struggle to get what they want. It's up to us to teach them that nothing is guaranteed, not even another day on this planet. It's up to us to teach them that money opens a lot of doors in their lives because everything we do costs. It's up to me to not let them believe the false narrative that money is the root of all evil when, in fact, money is completely neutral. As the guardians of the money we receive into our lives, we're the ones who can do harm or good with that money.

It's time to grow up and become an adult with our money. It's time to step into the challenges instead of shrinking away. It's time to make a budget. It's time to get out of debt. It's time to put down the glass of wine that tastes like "I have to go on Amazon and buy a cart full of stuff I don't need." It's time to invest. It's time to save. It's time to get out from under the pressure that money sometimes puts on us. Create a plan that is based on the things you value, and go about your life creating a reality around that dream. Look for more correlations between your work/business and financial fulfillment. Everything is connected, so find ways to overlap these cornerstones so that they are interwoven in a deeper way that keeps you focused. When it comes to relationships, find those trusted ones with a financial IQ that you can talk with and ask your financial questions to. Set a goal to become financially fit, and watch how that will impact your physical fitness and health. It's all connected; one good decision prepares you for the next good one.

You ready to put your finances through the WOOP experience?

WISH

CONTEMPLATE YOUR DEATH

What do you feel when you think about death and money?

When my mom died, she died in debt. She also had a poverty mindset that followed her right into that grave. That is not the story I want to take to the grave. I want to set myself up to be financially free for the rest of my life up to death. And here's why. I realized after she died how much her financial struggles impacted the enjoyment of her life. It always felt like she had a heavy stress burden on her shoulders, constantly worrying about next month. She was constantly finding reasons to not get too excited about anything in case the other shoe decided to drop due to her financial disarray, saying things like, "Expect a light Christmas" or "This won't last." That's not how I want to live my life. Paycheck to paycheck isn't going to work for me. So when I think about my death, I'm also forced to think about the quality of life leading up to that point.

If you were to die today, what would your finances look like?

How would you feel if you were to die with your finances in the state that they are in today?

Have you made a plan for your money in the event of your death?

Do you have life insurance so your death isn't a financial burden on your family?

Have you sat with your spouse and gone over what to do with your money if you both pass?

Are you in debt, and how would it feel to stay that way until death?

How would the people in your life feel about the way you lived it based on the financial situation you left behind?

What might you have been able to experience in your life if you had tackled your money problems right now rather than five, ten, or twenty years from now?

Do you feel like you've put everything you have into making enough money in your lifetime to experience all the things you want?

If you were to die today, is there anything you would have wished you'd done differently when it came to money?

DESIRE CHANGE

If you have a desire to change your money situation, it's probably a sign that your finances do need help. So it's good that you're ready to make the change. Are you ready to become financially independent and create wealth for yourself and your family? Are you tired of living in debt and barely making ends meet? You can change it, but the first step is having the desire to change.

OUTCOME

THINK FROM A SPIRITUAL PERSPECTIVE

There's a lot of conflicting information out there about what God thinks about money. Truth be told, money is a man-made object. Money is neither good nor bad; it's neutral. Again, there is no bad and there is no good. The way money is used can have either a positive or negative effect on our lives, that's true, but that's about our actions, not about the money. Money will not make you happy. Instead, money will reveal your priorities, values, and character. Fulfillment is not behind the next dollar. It's behind what you use that dollar to do in your life. I believe God wants us all to have the money to enhance our lives and fulfill our purpose. Whatever that purpose is for you, don't judge it. Don't put a label on it. Don't project your traumas or baggage onto your money. Definitely don't let others do that; I'd be dead broke if I let others put their financial baggage and mindsets on me. Money is neutral; it's up to you to do the good work with it.

Take some time to think about your preconceived beliefs or notions about money. Think about what creating wealth and removing financial stress from your life could do for your spirit. The lyrical poet Biggie Smalls once said, "mo money, mo problems," and that has become a common belief. I'm here to tell you that one of the worst feelings in the world was money stress for me. So, I don't necessarily agree. The truth is that the problems are just different. On one side you worry about being able to pay your mortgage if you don't have enough. On the other side, you worry about others trying to take it from you without earning it. Now that I've experienced both sides of the coin, being financially strapped and being financially free, I choose free. Every day I choose the freedom that financial independence brings.

I distinctly remember the feeling of being able to start a legit savings account. It was like a breath of fresh air not to have to worry if something happened and we needed an extra two thousand dollars right now. We began to start dreaming of what we could do with our money. One of the first things we did when we had enough saved was meet someone's need with it. I'll never forget the way that made me feel. When I was broke as a joke, I wouldn't have believed the feeling, but I promise you it feels like riding a unicorn. I can make a difference when I'm financially free in a way I couldn't otherwise.

CONNECT WITH YOUR VALUES

If you struggle financially, you have to connect the hard work of building wealth and financial fulfillment to something you truly value. Remember Andrea, who up and left her life behind to chase personal fulfillment? Do you think that was made easier or harder for her to do because she'd saved enough money to take the leap? Easier, of course. Money can make way for you to live within your values in all six cornerstones. She was able to live and pursue the things she really valued like independence and finding the meaning of life because she had first set aside the money to do so.

How can you create financial goals for yourself that help you live, act, and move in your highest values? Maybe you create milestones for yourself and rewards. Perhaps you connect your finances to the next level in the other five cornerstones of your good life. Discipline will come a lot easier if you know what you're working for and it's connected to the things you value.

OBSTACLE

Let's take the time to list out the obstacles, roadblocks, or challenges that might hold you back from your financial goals. I know people who have some mindset issues that stem from their strict religious upbringing. Let's call them the Smiths. It's interesting that many of those who cast stones about being wealthy are looking at it through the church lens. There's an undercurrent that runs through many churches that money is an evil thing. That can really affect your mindset if you believe it—so much so that your mind will get to work destroying your money so you don't have to have that evil thing around you, and that's exactly what is happening to the Smiths. Each month, they seem to find a way to end up back at zero dollars in the bank no matter how much is coming in, and y'all, they have a boatload of cheddar coming in, so much that it would make your eyes bleed to see the amount. They burn every dollar on things that don't matter or spend it on other people because, truthfully, they're good people and they love others. But they never seem to have enough to start saving for their future plans or to build any assets with their money. That's a mindset issue. They aren't responsible with a little money, just like they're not responsible with a lot. It doesn't matter if you make an hourly wage or a million bucks; your mindset will determine your ability to become wealthy.

Get yourself a mindset of wealth by thinking long-term about what might hold you back financially. Examine what you've been taught about money. Try to think back about what your parents believed about money, because you may believe the same things and not even realize it. Finally, examine what you might believe about people who are wealthy. If you hold negative beliefs about the kinds of people who are wealthy, you're going to have a hard time convincing your mind to want it. The same goes for your spouse. You and your spouse had better have a conversation about money, budgets, and all that surrounds money so you can get on the same page because it won't work if only one of you is committed.

> It doesn't matter if you make an hourly wage or a million bucks; your mindset will determine your ability to become wealthy.

Excuses are common when it comes to finances. Unless you're an accountant, it's likely that thinking about dollars, taxes, investments, and long-term plans doesn't rank high among the other cornerstones. *I can't because . . .* And our mind will believe what we tell it; remember the way we are wired.

Try journaling or listing the challenges you may come up against when it comes to financial fulfillment. And again, for those of you that do well with permissions, you can write them in a stream of consciousness or you can list them out, whatever works the best for you. Here are some possible questions to get you started.

- What obstacles are holding you back from the financial fulfillment you want in your life right now?
- How has your childhood or past colored the way you see and view money?
- What are your beliefs about how much is too much?
- What beliefs do you hold about being poor, and what might that say about you?
- What kinds of holdbacks in your life are going to complicate your financial situation?
- What is keeping you from being a magnet for money?
- What kind of financial obligations do you have that might make saving tough?
- What does your current budget look like, and is it working for you?

PLAN

DETERMINE YOUR ACTION PLAN

Finances are a struggle for most of us, which has created a lot of need and therefore has also created a lot of resources for this area. There are podcasts and videos coming out your ears that you can access for free online right now with a simple search. You can also try investing in a course to help you get on top of your finances; the money you spend to do it will keep you focused because you've actually invested in your growth. How about asking a bunch of questions to your accountant or CPA? There's an entire finances

section in every bookstore and library I've ever been in. **Make a plan**
It's never been easier to educate yourself on wealth with **to change**
the number of tools at your fingertips. Grab them, use **your mindset**
them, learn them. In truth, the thing you might need to **about money.**
learn about the most is yourself. Make a plan to change
your mindset about money. Be done being broke. Say
to yourself, *I'll never do that again.* Find a counselor to help you unpack the
things you don't know, understand, or see in yourself that might be keeping
you on the struggle bus. If you shop or spend for comfort, examine that.
Why? Try drilling down the feelings behind why spending money helps you
numb the uncomfortable feelings that discomfort invites into your mind.

Do what you need to do (journal, meditate, or draw) to ask yourself
the question, *What three things can I do right now to get me to my desired
new reality?*

CONNECT PLEASURE AND PAIN

This is the fun part. Take the time to do the Fortune 500 and Dickens
Process. Map out all the ways that having your finances in order is going
to be a good thing for you. Figure out why you even want money in your
life in the first place or it's never going to stay with you. Imagine the big life
you could live if you had the money to say yes to anything you feel called
to do. Trust me, the pleasure of not worrying about your finances should
be very high on that list. It's one of the accomplishments in my life that I
feel the proudest of, and that feeling has stuck with me longer than most.

GO TO WORK

Hundred-day challenge! How are you going to create a new habit and
mindset around money in one hundred days? Maybe you go on a contentment challenge where you don't buy anything for three months, like
my friend Kelly does about once a year. Maybe you decide you're going
to save a certain percentage of your income. Perhaps you create a budget
and stick to it for one hundred days. It is my guess that whatever habit you
create will end up being a part of your daily life without too much effort.

JUSTIFIABLE UNTRUTH IS STILL A LIE

HEALTH FULFILLMENT

A study conducted by HealthyWomen and *Working Mother* magazine revealed that women ranked their priorities and the time spent managing the health of those priorities in the following order:

1. Children
2. Pets
3. Elder relatives
4. Spouse or significant others
5. Themselves

Shockingly, 78 percent of the women surveyed said that they were so busy taking care of other family members' health that they put off taking care of themselves completely. Eighty-two percent of women do the majority of the health-related research for their kids, 86 percent schedule the majority of the healthcare appointments for their kids, and 72 percent of women arrange to pay the majority of the medical bills for their kids, which takes a considerable amount of time if insurance is involved.[1]

This was the area in which I had the hardest time finding consistent action. I tried every way I could think of to make a workout routine and healthy diet stick. The biggest problem I had is that I was focused on the wrong thing. When I'd hear health, I always assumed that meant physical body size. I had such issues around weight and worth that I didn't think of my health as anything other than how fat or how skinny I was. If I was skinny, I was healthy. If I was fat, I was not. And the diet industry was very happy for me to keep believing that. They were preying on my low self-worth and misunderstanding of health.

No wonder I couldn't make an extreme diet stick. No wonder I would lose a little followed by gaining it back plus some. No wonder I didn't want to think about my "health." No wonder I felt out of control, unskilled, and unable to make changes last. I was focused on the outside and not the inside.

My desire to finally make my body, mind, soul, and spirit healthy came at a time when things weren't great in my marriage. We were struggling, and I had this moment of clarity where I realized Michael could never love me the way I wanted him to because I didn't love myself that way. I realized that in order for me to truly feel fulfilled in my life, I couldn't ignore myself any longer. I mean shocker, right? But I can feel some of you having a lightbulb moment as I type this. I started by changing my mind first by going to see a counselor to help me work out my inner baggage and trauma. I started listening to the signals my body and mind were sending me about what could be. For so long I had learned to completely zone out the signals my body would send me. Hunger, pain, feelings, stress, outbursts, annoyances, problems—I ignored them all. Honestly, I didn't know not to. I thought that's what we did to get things done. You ignore it.

I bought a yoga mat and decided to focus on inner peace and joy through movement and concentration. I decided to stop worrying about the size of my body and focus on something I could change, like starting and completing something difficult for me. I concentrated on being a good example for my three daughters. I concentrated on changing the way I felt about my body instead of changing my body to fit some standard of beauty. I did it because what I wanted was to stay alive. I had a lot to live for. I knew I had to change, and in order for me to get what I wanted out of the other five cornerstones of a good life, I had to have a working mind and body. And I had a lot of plans for the other parts of my life.

> I concentrated on changing the way I felt about my body instead of changing my body to fit some standard of beauty.

When I set my intentions on getting control of my health, it was the scariest and biggest goal I'd ever set. My intention was to make my health a priority, something I had never connected to in the past. It was not a priority or a value in my life, so I had some major blocks to overcome.

Sitting in a seminar in California, I did both the Fortune 500 exercise and the Dickens Process. I didn't just do it halfway; I played full-out that day, and I did it all. I let myself feel all of the amazing and fulfilling results that would come from that Fortune 500 exercise. I sat in what those wins would feel like. I let the emotion show on my face. I convinced my mind to act.

I then went right into the Dickens Process and sat in how it would feel to avoid the change. I played the declining health game with myself until I saw my death. I imagined what my kids would say and how they would feel. I imagined my husband finding another wife to replace me and raise my kids. I felt the pain I would be inflicting on the people I know and claim to love. I sat in it and cried (like, ugly cried) as I imagined my kids realizing I didn't care enough about myself to prevent early death. I sat in the feeling that they would be absolutely right. I let the tears come. I let them hurt.

Change came about seven months later. It felt terrible for three of those months because working out hurts; it takes up time in the day; I can list a thousand things I'd rather be doing with my time that are much more comfortable. Change just feels uncomfortable, but remember, that struggle is for you in the long run. Finally, one day the clouds parted, and I created a habit of taking care of myself without the stress that usually accompanies that action. I didn't do anything but consistently show up and move my body in a way that felt good that day, and the habit formed around that consistency. I found myself without an excuse to run away from the gym. I found myself being pushed into the thing I had convinced my mind to want. I no longer wake up and feel like gym time is the bane of my existence. I wake up and put on workout clothes right away. I don't skip the gym because it's important and it leads me closer to fulfillment, and my mind knows it.

One night while sitting in a beautiful NYC restaurant, Michael and I started a conversation about death. It's good to think about death every day. Get used to it; embrace it so you don't have to fight against something you absolutely, positively will have to face one day. That particular night, it took no time for my mind to serve me up the age of fifty-three. Since my mom died at this age, I just assumed that would be when I'd go too. Family history and all. It took me about thirteen seconds to realize how little time I had left to do all the things I wanted to do in my life. No, fifty-three cannot be right. Fourteen years isn't enough.

My next question was, *If I wanted to live longer than my mom to experience more of what life has to offer, could I do that?* The amazing thing about asking yourself pointed questions is that you'll get pointed answers. Yes, I knew instantly, there would be a way to prolong my life, but it wouldn't happen by accident. You can't lazy your way through life and find yourself at the age of ninety-eight.

> You can't lazy your way through life and find yourself at the age of ninety-eight.

I knew that my level of adulting would directly correlate to the length of my life. In other words, if I wanted to stay alive to the age of ninety-eight, I'd have to try to stay alive on purpose. The excuses had to stop. The action had to start. And most importantly, my mindset had to change.

In mere seconds it felt as if I had a new direction and vigor because I reminded myself that if I wanted to do the things I claim to love and are important to me, I had to be alive. I never thought about staying alive on purpose. I more thought of it as a thing that was or was not—something beyond my control. And, in part, I was right. Some of my being alive or dead is beyond my control, but what I can control, I was ignoring. My food intake was poor and feelings-based. My workout habits were stationary to sedentary at best. My vigor for life went as far as my next goal but no further. And I justified it all by saying something we have all said, "I don't have time."

But I knew that was a lie.

A lie I could justify, but justifiable untruth is still a lie. The worst part is that I was lying to myself, the one person who knew without a doubt it was false. I continued to lie to a person who knew I was lying to them, and I had no choice but to live with myself anyway. Those lies became so easy to live with and I, myself, never realized that each time I said some kind of untruth I was betraying myself. I was becoming less and less trustworthy to myself. I'd pride myself on truth to others and then lie directly to my own face. That's wrong. Our number one priority should be ourselves, but we'll never trust ourselves until we start getting honest about absolutely everything.

Recently I've been diving into the idea of seeing my true self and asking her what she wants—not the me that is perceived, accepted, or rejected by others. Not who I want to be or wish to be. Not who my parents raised me to be. I want to connect with my spirit. My spirit is me as the observer of my life. She's not my body, and she's not my mind. She's the me that is unaffected by emotions, the past, success, others, and perceptions. She's unaffected by praise just as she is unaffected by hate. I want to build a life that works for me, but that means identifying, unpacking, and facing anything I've outgrown or that no longer serves me. It means figuring out what I was taught and what I actually believe.

So I decided to get honest about the kind of life that I wanted to live and the kind of life I was capable of creating. I want to be the mom who runs with her kids. I want to be the wife who's confident in her skin and wants her husband to see all of her. I want to be healthy enough to have all adventures on the table because I have enough energy to pursue them. I realized that I can't do all the things I feel called to or excited by if I don't take care of my body and mind. If I wanted to live past fifty-three, I had to do something and I had to do something now. One thing I know about myself is that if I connect strongly enough to a goal or outcome, I can achieve absolutely anything I set my mind to.

> While change can happen overnight, results take a little longer.

I've proven that to myself over and over again, just as you will. I needed to work that desire into one of my core values and I had to get enough leverage on myself to make the change stick.

I also needed time and patience. While change can happen overnight, results take a little longer. Am I willing to hang on for the long run for this?

Let's do that WOOP experience on our health, shall we?

WISH

CONTEMPLATE YOUR DEATH

If you let your health issues go on for the rest of your life without making the effort to correct them, how long do you have left? Who's at your funeral watching your lifeless body being lowered into the ground? What are your kids and spouse feeling? How is this loss going to affect them? What kind of example were you for the people who looked up to you in life about the importance of taking care of your mind, body, soul, and spirit?

DESIRE CHANGE

Do you want to change something about the way you're taking care of yourself? Is there something you know you need to change urgently because it's becoming a problem in your life? Do you want more for your health, but you struggle to stay consistent? All you need for this step is the desire to change your habits and conditioning.

ADMIT THERE'S MORE

I hear a lot of excuses about working out, and look, I get it. I've been there, done that, and I'm writing the book about it. I hear a lot of excuses about prepping and eating healthy food. I get that too. Your excuses are valid. Most of us always stay asleep to our life. That's your option, too, but now you know better. Is there more in the tank for you? Do you have another level in you that allows you to prioritize your health? Is there room for you to dedicate some time and effort to your health?

OUTCOME

THINK FROM A SPIRITUAL PERSPECTIVE

When you're quiet, what does your spirit say to you about how you're taking care of yourself? How much effort are you putting into your health? What do you feel pulled to do? I found yoga because it was a way that I could move my body and take care of it while also taking care of my mind. We're all different. Your spirit is leading you to a way to take care of yourself that works for you. What outcome are you looking for? Is it just to look good for others? Is it to make your body last as long as you can? I changed my goals from losing weight to getting stronger and more flexible, and it has made a huge difference in my effort simply because my spirit connects to that kind of goal.

CONNECT WITH YOUR VALUES

Take a look at the things you value in your life. How can you incorporate movement and healthy foods into those values? For example, I highly value my children and the relationship I have with them. I want to teach them good habits when they're young so they don't struggle to take care of their bodies like I have. I can make menu-planning and getting into the gym every day a priority by connecting it to the health of my children. My kids look up to me. They follow me in every way they can right now. It's adorable. It's also a lot of responsibility. They're watching me. They're taking their cues for action from me. I want them to see me make health a priority. It's easier for me to get my butt in the gym and make a meal with healthy ingredients when I realize my actions are connected to that value.

You do the same for yourself. Find ways to connect the thing you really find yourself resisting to the things you cannot resist.

OBSTACLE

When it comes to eating right and working out, the list of obstacles is easy for me to generate. Just as easy as it is for me to order a coffee, I can list one hundred obstacles for why I can't do the thing I know I should right now. Ninety-nine percent of those obstacles are me. I am the biggest roadblock to my success when it comes to my health. I'm solely responsible for my body and mind. If I don't make it a priority, it cannot be done by someone else. A lot of the resistance around taking care of ourselves comes from self-worth issues.

We feel ugly and fat in our physical bodies, so we stay out of the gym so people don't see us. Side note: they're looking at their phones or themselves in the mirror, not you. We aren't strong enough to nail a workout on the first try, so we never go back. We expect things of our bodies that we have no business expecting so that we can keep ourselves small and safe and out of sight of others. We are wearing our shame on our body. Until we learn to love ourselves more than we're worried about what others think, nothing will change.

> Until we learn to love ourselves more than we're worried about what others think, nothing will change.

My physical transformation this year is pretty dramatic. I look different in my skin now, and that's really just a reflection of my inner world showing on the outside. I posted a photo of the transformation on my social media profile (@lindsayteague) so people could see what I was talking about.[2]

But I had to make myself do it. I was so scared to post it, not because I give a rip what anyone thinks about my body now but because I don't want my physical body to be a conversation someone has with themself that goes something like this:

"Oh man, I look worse than her 'before' picture" or "I'll just obsess over food and the scale" or, even worse, "Must be nice"—which keeps a person stuck forever.

I chose to show the physical transformation because I can't show the mental one. But the mental one is what I want to talk about. My transformation is not a physical victory. This is a mental victory for the me before action. She figured this out! My physical body almost doesn't matter (outside of my own beliefs about it), but it sure does get attention, doesn't it? When I share photos of my body, I hope to use that attention to have these kinds of conversations with people.

If you want a physical transformation, you won't get it by pushing your body to its limits in the gym for two-a-days. You won't get it by joining the bros in the who-can-throw-weights-the-hardest contests. You won't get it through an eating disorder, for God's sake. You won't. Skinny and sick as hell is not a victory.

The key to the physical transformation is the mental transformation. It doesn't matter how hard you hate yourself into a gym or how hard you hate yourself into a diet. That hate will not stick. To love yourself into transformation, you must love the you on day one. Don't love yourself? Don't think you're beautiful? Don't think you're worthy? These are the inner parts you'll need to contend with before you try to work out your body. My advice is that you seek a therapist before the gym.

It's a new mindset. It's believing in your worth. Only a person who values themself spends time loving themself into the gym and loving themself into a healthy body and mind. That hate you keep giving

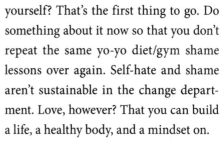

Face yourself and fix your mindset now. You can. It is the biggest obstacle standing between you and your health.

yourself? That's the first thing to go. Do something about it now so that you don't repeat the same yo-yo diet/gym shame lessons over again. Self-hate and shame aren't sustainable in the change department. Love, however? That you can build a life, a healthy body, and a mindset on.

Face yourself and fix your mindset now. You can. It is the biggest obstacle standing between you and your health.

PLAN

DETERMINE YOUR ACTION PLAN

What do you need to do to start taking care of your mind, body, soul, and spirit? Is it really just your body? Do you need to focus on self-love or empathy? What kinds of things have you been saying to yourself over the last decade or more to keep yourself stuck in shame and fear? What do you need to do right now to stop that shit and start loving yourself?

CONNECT PLEASURE AND PAIN

If you find yourself with major blocks that have held you back from the kind of change you desire so badly, it might be a good idea to do both the Fortune 500 and Dickens Process. For me, I had to dig deep to get this kind of work to stick to me. I had to really, really try to change my mindset about what I was seeing in the mirror and who I wanted to be. I had to create a neural network around my health success that didn't allow me to bail on myself again. Take these activities seriously and let the weight of all your feeling settle on you.

I'm sounding the alarm. It's time to shift *right now*. This process will kick your ass in the best way possible if you let it. If you struggle with body image, self-love, movement, or eating food that nourishes your body, you need to do both exercises. Enough is enough. It's time to wake up and get to work.

GO TO WORK

Let's hundred-day challenge this! This challenge was so good for me on so many levels. I set a goal to work out every day for one hundred days and as soon as my first hundred was up, I started the next because it just felt right. This habit isn't hard for me to keep up any longer. I'm struggling more to keep up with healthy habits around meditation right now. The gym is my friend now, all because of this hundred-day challenge. See what happens when you challenge yourself to something that feels impossible. I promise you won't find yourself on day ninety-nine saying, "Welp, this was a huge waste of time and energy." You'll probably be saying something like, "What else can I do to push myself further?" Remember, you make the rules on this challenge. The real prize is knowing you made it and that you have the personal power to do a hard thing for one hundred days in a row. If you can do that, you can certainly make your health a priority a few times a week for the rest of your life.

GO MANIFEST WHAT YOU WANT IN YOUR LIFE

RELATIONSHIP FULFILLMENT

There are three primary relationship types I want to focus on when it comes to setting goals for your good life. That's not to say there won't be other relationships that are important to you, but I have found that these three types of relationships tend to be the most important across the board. They are your marriage, your friendships, and your family relationships. Each requires separate focus and will likely not all be the same priority for you.

Connections and relationships with other people are an integral part of a good life. We are meant to learn from one another. We are meant to affect one another. We have so much we can give to help one another as we pursue the idea of a good life.

If you struggle with relationships as I have, this is a lesson for you. If you find yourself longing for others to share your authentic life with, this is important for you to read. If you find yourself with too many relationships that stay on the surface, I've got you covered too. You're meant to read this today.

YOUR RELATIONSHIP TARGET

I like to think of my relationships as a target.[1] In the center are the people who are the closest to me—my relationships with my husband and my kids, plus there's space for a very special friendship or two. The center dot of the target is special and important. Getting into that dot isn't easy, and getting out of it is going to prove difficult as well. I set up a lot of defenses around this circle. Thou shalt not eff with my inner circle. I will not have it, and I'm willing to make a scene to prove it. You come after my family, you better bring a gun, because I ain't bringing a knife. It's like that.

The next circle in the target is for the friends whom I love but may not interact with on a daily basis. These people are the kinds of friends you want to go with on a girls' trip or even yearly vacations. They're family friends that you get together with to let the kids play. They're the extended family. You may include the people you go to lunch with each day at work in this list. You may include neighbors in this list. The second ring is filled with people who make you laugh and you have a good time with.

You offer them what you have, and they offer you the same back. If any of these people need something from me, I'm going to be there. As long as the relationship is mutually beneficial, they'll stay in that ring for me. But if these people need more time than I'm giving to the inner circle, we're going to have to have a conversation at some point. Should they begin to demand more or the equitable exchange of energy becomes unbalanced, you'll find them drifting farther and farther from that center circle. Sometimes that happens because of distance or time, but usually it happens because time changes things and what was of high value to you at one point may not be as important now.

You're going to outgrow some people who are in your life right now. Letting them go will often feel elitist and wrong. Keeping them in your life when the relationship is no longer serving one of the parties isn't right for either side, but we do it because having the talk or making the decision to put our energy into a different friend isn't comfortable. Don't fight the process; learn through it. Notice the feelings. Notice the responses.

Here's the thing about relationships: there's a right number of them for each of us, and none of us are the same. My best friend in the entire world for the last twenty-two years has been the same person. I've had about three close friends at a time throughout my life, and she's consistently had five or more at times. She needs more friends in her circle than I do, and that's totally okay with us. She has taught me more than any friend I've ever had. She has stuck with me longer than any friend I've ever had, and I'm not one of those friends who avoids change. I thrive in change. The other day, Kelly said of me, "I don't really know what Lindsay would say yes to right now" because I change my mind and am open to change more than most people. I'm hard to keep up with. Kelly might well be the only person on my friends list who consistently shows up in the place where I'm changing. For most, it's too uncomfortable, and I can understand that. The truth is, Kelly loves the part of me that enjoys and gets excited about change. That's part of who she is as well. We go about acquiring and experiencing change through different things, but our ability to welcome change is one of the things that makes us compatible.

Just yesterday, I sat in her backyard as we talked about the changes in my life. We had a State of the Union-style discussion where we both reiterated the importance of our friendship and where we both stated what we wanted from each other and what we didn't. We talked about potential underlying issues and the things that might prevent us from being as close as we are now in the future. These are the kinds of talks you should be having with the people who are in your inner circle. It's not the kind of honesty most people have in their friendships because most of them aren't deep connections, which we settle for because they're safe. If you don't have these kinds of discussions, you're not getting honest enough together. And that kind of connection or chemistry is what you need to survive friendship. I learned that from Kelly. She raised me in the friend department. I give in different ways, of course, but she showed me what was possible, and we need that in our lives.

I'm willing to bend over backward for her to feel the love I have for her. If that means meeting her where she's at and giving to her in a new way, that's what it means. She would do the same for me. That's why she continues to be in my inner circle. She's, in fact, the only other person in that circle beyond my husband or kids. I have set my mind on making this friendship last, and that means she gets more work than some of my other relationships. Making some of your connections a priority over others isn't mean or self-serving; it's required.

Find people in your life who will consistently prove to you that there's more. Attach yourself to the kind of person who will show you that the real good stuff is beyond your threshold of success, that it's deeper than you think, that more is required, and it won't be easy, but it will be worth it. People like Kelly get a *hell yes* from me because they deserve it. I receive so much from the relationship, I'm willing to say *hell yes* to make sure

> Find people in your life who will consistently prove to you that there's more.

she's receiving the same from me. I will work to make sure this friendship survives because it's of high value to me. Fight for those friends.

The final circle is the outer ring. This is where I place the people who I simply know: coworkers, friends for a reason, colleagues, friends of friends, people I interact with through temporary small groups, and so on. You're likely not taking advice on really difficult or vulnerable problems in your life with your outer circle. They just don't know you like that, and you don't know them like that. If you ever find yourself giving more of yourself to your outer circle than your inner circle, that's a really good indication that you've got your priorities screwed up.

I want you to take some time to fill out this target with the people in your life. For some of you, you'll need more room for names. Again, this isn't a popularity contest. You don't win anything for having the most people on your target. Too many people on this list can easily keep you from the other five cornerstones of a good life if you aren't careful. I find relationships is the place where you can get yourself caught up in time-sucks, especially when it comes to high-maintenance or needy relationships—the ones who always find a reason to need you. And if there is an unhealed part of you that longs to be needed or to rescue others, you have a recipe for disaster. You'll know if that's you because you're always the clean-up crew and that same level of interest seems to be missing when you're in need. Pay attention to the signs.

The Relationship Target

We're going to walk through each of the three relationship categories and create some visions of what a fulfilling relationship might feel like with them. We're going to create a few lists of things you want to do with those people and how you want to experience a relationship with them. When you're ready to take on the relationships in your life as a priority, these exercises will be here to help guide you.

THE FRIENDSHIP WOOP EXPERIENCE

WISH

CONTEMPLATE YOUR DEATH

Imagine your death. Imagine you're looking up from your grave. Who is there? What are they saying about you that's real? What are they saying about you that's not true? How do they feel about your loss? How will your friends remember you? How do things change without you in the lives of your friends? Seeing what you've accomplished in the friend department, are there things you know you need to change? What was missing in your experiences with your friends that would have led you to more meaningful experiences while you were alive? Do the people who claim you as a friend truly know and love you? Have you truly known and loved them?

DESIRE CHANGE

What more are you wishing for as far as your friendships are concerned? What kind of changes in your friendships would lead to greater fulfillment in your life? How might you be able to become the friend you're longing for in your life?

OUTCOME

THINK FROM A SPIRITUAL PERSPECTIVE

Check in with your spirit. What does your internal voice tell you is going on with your relationships with friends? Is there an outcome that you are desiring that is not in the cards with the friendships you have right now? How are you connecting with the friends you have on a spiritual level? When was the last time you had a conversation that was vulnerable and raw with your friends that leaves you feeling filled up and supported? Do you feel like your friends really see you? What might it feel like to have a group of friends who you know are in your corner supporting the person you're discovering is within you? What kinds of outcomes are you hoping to avoid in your friendships?

CONNECT WITH YOUR VALUES

Look back at your list of values for your life. What kinds of people or experiences are missing in your friend relationships that would move you closer to those values?

The best way to make sure a friendship is going to work through conflicting values is to be honest right up front about who you are and what kind of a friend you'll be. I used to wish myself into different values so that I could keep "safe" relationships. I would sign up for regular phone calls or for meetups with groups that just weren't my cup of tea because I thought I might be able to change my mind about what fulfills me. But I can't, so I started being honest, and my friendships are so much more satisfying. Boundaries are important. Draw yours and allow your friends to draw theirs. If it works, it will flow. If it doesn't, that may be a sign that you need to reevaluate the time and energy you're putting into a relationship that just doesn't fit quite right. That doesn't mean you can't be friends or you have to be mad at that person. It just means that perhaps that relationship is meant to be a little farther from the bullseye on the target. Perhaps you both are meant to affect the lives of other people at this time. That doesn't have to be a bad thing. Keep relationships that actually work.

> The best way to make sure a friendship is going to work through conflicting values is to be honest right up front about who you are and what kind of a friend you'll be.

OBSTACLE

What are a few of the obstacles that could stand in the way of you having fulfilling friendships in your life? Some common friendship obstacles are:

- Differences in core values
- Other relationships causing strain
- Distance (physical or emotional)
- Social media driving disconnection
- Fear of intimacy with a friend
- Overly packed schedules
- Insecurities creating possessiveness or jealousy
- Secrets or trust issues
- Competition fueling disconnection

PLAN

DETERMINE YOUR ACTION PLAN

Ask yourself what actions you need to take to move your current reality from what it is to what you want it to become. You must believe it's possible for this to work. If the current picture is what is real to you right now, what things do you need to do to set yourself on a path to the future picture?

Think and meditate on this, then draw what your friendship situation feels like to you if you need help working through this section. And ask yourself, *What three things can I do right now that will get me closer to the reality I desire in my life?* That should give you enough of a vision for your friendships to move you on to the next step.

CONNECT PLEASURE AND PAIN

There is likely one of these actions you know you need to take but it scares the bejeezus out of you. First of all, right on. Second, that's the one I want you to focus on. The most radical and scary action is guaranteed to produce results. It will either feel really good or really bad, but either way, it's the correct way to feel because it is reality. Don't fight reality on this change process. Do the Fortune 500 exercise and list all of the pleasure you can think of. Think about why this action is no longer an available option but is now a requirement to change. Convince yourself with enough data to start working toward fulfillment through friendship.

If you'd rather, you can always run your friendships through the Dickens Process. Imagine your life if it continues relationally as it is now. What happens if you give up on seeking meaningful relationships in your life? What kind of adventures or fun might you miss out on? How would it feel to have only a few people show up for your funeral because you were never able to get yourself into a place where you were that friend for someone else? What kind of life are you living without friends to share it with?

If you find yourself paralyzed by fear in this area, you likely have some people-pleasing work to do and some self-acceptance work to do. Your fulfillment will never be the thing that every relationship in your life wants for you. Your fulfillment lands squarely on your shoulders to provide for yourself. It will never be a part of your relationships if you continue to settle for crappy ones that don't work for you. You're worth more than that as a friend, and your friends deserve more than a friend who's half in.

GO TO WORK

Now it's time to go to work. Start making moves. Start taking action. Write down the goals you have for your friendships and then get your ass kicked all over the place as you become the friend who deserves those kinds of fulfilling friendships. Start writing what you want to attract on pieces of paper. Start talking about what you're looking for. Start praying for it. Create for yourself a hundred-day challenge to connect with a friend of yours you truly value.

A couple of years ago, I was sitting in an auditorium filled with four thousand women. At one point, I started to pray for someone new to come into my life. Someone new in all ways. I wanted someone who didn't look like me, who didn't talk like me. I wanted someone who didn't think like me. I wanted someone who would teach me about parts of the world I wasn't yet familiar with. I wanted someone to come into my life who could help me open my eyes to something new, and I wanted to do the same for that person. I wasn't looking for a friend who could entertain me or give me anything. I just wanted them to stimulate my thoughts, and I wanted to do the same in return. I wanted a rich friendship that would be equal parts giving and receiving in multifaceted ways I didn't even know were possible. I wanted the new inspiring conversations that would come from a friendship like that. A friendship where we would feel like two little girls, swapping binoculars and experiencing new insight from our different vantage points.

My friend Yoshika landed in my path within months of setting my intentions in motion. When she showed up in my life, I went out of my way to ask her to be my friend. I asked her for her phone number, which is out of my character, and I made my feelings about her known. I gave her my phone number and told her, "I want to be your friend," like I was back in elementary school. What worked then still works now. What's the worst that could happen, she doesn't call me? Okay, I can handle that. I have to take responsibility to find the relationships I want in my life to fulfill this part of my life. I didn't wait for her to pursue me. I pursued her friendship. That friendship has turned into something amazing over the last couple of years. She's exactly what I was looking for, and I'm convinced I found her because I went looking for her. She was on my radar since that day I prayed for her. I manifested her!

Do that. Go manifest what you want in your life. But you better be ready to step up to the plate for that relationship. You will be forced to become the person who can sustain a high-level friendship if you ask for it. You will be required to become an attentive friend if that's what you're craving. You will be forced to face your own baggage if you want a friendship built without trauma bonds. Be prepared to become what you're after. The friend you're thinking about deserves the wholehearted version of you, and it's likely they aren't going to settle for a whole lot less. Quality demands quality.

> **You will be forced to face your own baggage if you want a friendship built without trauma bonds.**

MARRIAGE

Side note: this section is for those who are married or want to be (if this is not for you, feel free to proceed without caution). I believe that if you're not married but would like to be, then learning now from this kind of noted experience will only set you up and ready you for this future goal.

In the last two years, Michael and I have seen a huge shift in our marriage, and it has contributed to my fulfillment in a way I have a hard time putting into words. I've been married to Michael Moreno for thirteen years. We've had an amazing marriage, and I don't just say that so you'll think we're awesome. Of course, we've had ups and downs. Sometimes when emotions are high, we hurt each other, but we always work it out together eventually.

A couple of years ago, as I looked down the road at my marriage to Michael, I knew we'd be happy. We'd like each other. We probably would have made it work throughout our lives because we're compatible like that, but I also saw that there was an ability for us to be closer, more connected. There were tiny holes we had created in our relationship that we never went back to fix. Tiny holes created by words unsaid, fights not finished, hurts we'd given each other, and desires unspoken. I saw that with some work, there was another level in there for us as a couple and that we could grow together to create a marriage that was truly excellent.

I wanted better than good. I wanted better than great. I wanted excellence. I wanted partnership that I was proud of in the good times and the challenging times. I wanted the kind of relationship I hoped my daughters would have with their spouses one day. And I realized, if I wanted it for my daughters, then I damn well wanted it for myself. How can I expect my kids to push for more if I am not willing? You can never desire for others the things you think you don't deserve. It doesn't work like that. Nobody else is responsible for your happiness and fulfillment but you.

In order for me to push for more in our marriage, I had to be willing to let go of the great marriage we already had. I was willing for him to say to me, "You're not worth this" or "I can't meet you where you are right now." I was willing to let him walk away because I wanted more in my marriage, even if he decided he didn't. *What if I want more and Michael decides that it's just too much work? What if the next level isn't something he can see? What if he's not ready for that kind of personal development? What if I'm not worth that work for him? What if he's already tired from what he does for our family, which admittedly is a lot? What if this breaks us?* I was willing to explore those what-ifs in real life.

I had to wrestle with these kinds of questions before I presented him with the idea of more. And we're talking about a good marriage, a marriage that I loved. A man I wanted and needed. A relationship that was really important to me—the most important to me, actually.

In the end, I decided that my fulfillment and joy were worth facing any relationship challenges, even the ones that come with wanting more out of a good marriage. I need a marriage that is excellent because I believe it's possible. I believed in our relationship and our ability to mold and improve ourselves into something even more beautiful. I've seen amazing marriage examples throughout my life, which proved to me it was possible. And if it's possible for one couple, it's possible for me and it's possible for you.

So, I got out a box of matches, sat down with my husband, and asked him for more. I told him I wanted more sex, more intimacy, to know him inside and out, to be known completely, and that what we had was nice, but it wasn't enough for me. I lit that match and set the house on fire. For a while, when we were watching what we used to be burn, I felt terrible. All of those voices in my head that say, "You're not worth this" and "Look what you did now" came to play. One day I sat in my depression and sadness, and I was so afraid I had made a huge mistake. *Is this what self-sabotage feels like? You took a perfectly good thing and threw it out the window because you just can't be happy, Lindsay. You're doing it again. See, this is your problem. You did this.* Ever been there?

And things got bad for a couple of months as we adjusted and went to work on ourselves. We were fighting more, we were butting heads, and we felt alone a lot. Some days we'd feel resentment toward each other for growing on different timelines. Sometimes we had different ideas about what a happy marriage looked like. Unlearning the stories we've told ourselves about our lives is really soul-wrenching work. It truly does feel like a form of grief to give the older version of your relationship up so you can start over. I was risking something I deeply loved for an idea I wasn't even sure we could achieve. Why?

Because my spirit knew it was there.

I knew it in my heart. My spirit told me something deeper was there over and over again for a few years. When I closed my eyes I could see us at that next level. I could see a partnership with Michael that didn't carry baggage around and wasn't based on using each other to get our highest needs met. We just never thought to take all the baggage (past hurts, regrets, experiences, and traumas) we brought into our marriage and set it down before we started our relationship. Instead we existed together with our past baggage tainting our view of what actually was and what could be.

Think back. Has there been a time in your life when you knew something more and better was out there for you? Maybe it was taking the leap to leave a job that was secure but wasn't fulfilling. Maybe you left a relationship that you knew didn't have that next level in it. Perhaps you took a risk on something you just knew was the right move for you, but others didn't understand. Maybe you asked for the promotion or the raise. Or maybe it was as simple as asking for a favor from a friend, which can be difficult for some of us.

That feeling? That's your Spidey sense tingling. Your spirit is trying to get your attention. That's the part of you connected to God. He whispers into that part of you and puts options on the table for you to explore. You can certainly ignore it. I did for a while with Michael. I wasn't ready to risk it. I didn't want to hurt his feelings. I didn't think I was worth it. But my spirit kept pulling the string, and eventually that pull became the song of my heart. I couldn't escape the idea that it was possible to build a stronger marriage that could withstand any storm. And I mean any storm. I used the examples of amazing partnerships that I'd seen throughout my life as proof that it was possible, and I let myself believe it.

I realized that what I wanted most out of my relationship with my husband was to be fully known and loved anyway. I decided to take some action by telling him my secrets. Remember that I grew up in a house of secrets. That was standard operating procedure for me, and I realized it was also toxic operating procedure. And that decision set me on a path to know and love myself first. I didn't want to pretend anymore. No more hiding both physically and emotionally. I wanted him to see me, really see me with all of my faults, terrible choices, self-sabotage, and too-muchness. And I wanted him to choose me, but if he didn't or couldn't, I was willing to choose myself. Unlearning secret-keeping has been so difficult because brutal honesty about the things I'm not proud of in my story feels wrong at times. The more I grow, the easier it gets. The more I change my mindset about negative experiences, the more I see them as stepping-stones and not disqualifications.

As I went to work on accepting myself just as I am, the more willing I was to put the real me in front of my husband. His acceptance was no longer a requirement for my own acceptance. That's a strange feeling when you've been conditioned to believe that you can only love the lovable parts of yourself. I went so far as to let him in on some of the secrets I was sure I'd take to the grave with me. You know the ones that have nothing to do with him and reveal me in a not-so-favorable light? Those stories.

> **I realized that what I wanted most out of my relationship with my husband was to be fully known and loved.**

I decided to just start telling him my story. All of my story. The things I thought other people wouldn't want or need to know. I told him the things that hurt the most. I told him honestly how parts of my story made me feel. Mostly, I shared my emotions with him, something I had hidden way down deep inside myself. I shared all the things I thought would make someone run away from me. I held my relationship with him in an open hand. I was going to be honest, and he could choose to stay and love me or go. It was his choice, and I realized how little it had to do with me.

At one point I realized that for the first eleven years of our marriage I kept a part of my heart and soul from Michael. Not because he hadn't earned it, not because he had given me a reason to distrust him, and not because I didn't want to give it to him. I didn't even know I was in protection mode at the beginning of our relationship.

Until I opened my eyes and woke up.

I got tired of my own bullshit (sensing a theme here yet?), and I went all in with Michael. I allowed him to see me both physically and emotionally without shame. And that little emotional switch caused Michael to do the same. Suddenly, we are getting to know each other in a totally new way, a decade into marriage. We're connecting in a way that allows the other to see our decisions, choices, or challenges in a new light. We are doing it!

Because Michael knows I grew up in a household where emotions were perceived as negative, he can understand when my first reaction is to quiet my emotions and feel some shame around them. Because Michael knows how drastically my relationship to my mother had changed in my adult years, he can better understand the brand of grief I am feeling over losing her to a massive heart attack at the age of fifty-three. Because I know Michael grew up in extreme poverty and often felt unseen as a kid, I can understand his reactions and emotions better. Because I know Michael's history, I understand his triggers and I can identify quickly what kind of support he may need in the moment.

Telling your stories as an adult gives you the chance to find out what's really true and what was actually just your mind preparing you for survival. Telling your stories allows you to reexperience those feelings from a more knowledgeable and mature place to make sense of them. Telling your stories gives you a chance to let them go. It allows you to strike a match and burn the old ones that no longer serve you in your life. You don't live there anymore.

> Telling your stories as an adult gives you the chance to find out what's really true and what was actually just your mind preparing you for survival.

This change in my marriage has made way for an entirely new relationship between my husband and myself. In the past year we've learned that we don't need each other; we've chosen, instead, to want to be together. It's no longer me versus him when shit hits the fan. It's him and me versus the problem. There's nothing I can't tell him and there's nothing he can't tell me. Have we told each other everything? Of course not. We have a lot of life yet to live. And we plan to live it with arms wide open and hearts exposed.

Are you ready for a rock-solid marriage? Are you hoping for a marriage that fulfills you and leaves room for who you really are and who you will become? Let's take our desires and hopes for our marriage and drag them through the WOOP experience.

THE MARRIAGE WOOP EXPERIENCE

WISH

CONTEMPLATE YOUR DEATH

Imagine looking up from your grave at your spouse. How did it end? What kinds of things did you never say or do? What grade would you give yourselves for the marriage you had so far? Were there unrealized dreams on the table for your marriage that are still sitting there? Were you proud of the marriage you created?

DESIRE CHANGE

What do you wish your marriage looked like? What are you hoping for? What do you believe it has the potential to feel like? What feelings are missing from your current marriage situation? What needs are not being met in your marriage? What kinds of things do you want to experience in your marriage? What does your sex life look like right now, and what could it look like? How are you speaking about your marriage with your friends and family? How are you being treated behind the closed doors of your home? What things need to change? What could help change the way you feel about working on your marriage right now? What kinds of adventures do you hope to have with your spouse? How equal are the two of you when it comes to duties around the house? What kinds of things do you regularly find yourselves fighting about? How likely are you to go find yourself support as you change your mind-set about your marriage?

OUTCOME

THINK FROM A SPIRITUAL PERSPECTIVE

What messages are you continually getting from your spirit that lead you to believe there's another level in your marriage out there for you? Think of yourself as a child dreaming of a fantasy marriage. What kinds of things are missing from that initial list that are still important to you? When you're still and quiet, what kinds of messages do you receive about your marriage?

CONNECT WITH YOUR VALUES

Connect the outcome you want for your marriage to your core values. How will a fulfilling marriage help you move toward living a life that you value? If your spirit is calling you to work on your marriage, there's a good chance that there's buried treasure in this relationship. You've just got to locate it and go to work.

OBSTACLE

Our ability to overcome obstacles is always right there, in our mindset. To deal with obstacles and to convince your mind of the importance of what you want in your life, you need to reinforce how important it is to you. You can do one exercise, or you can do both. If you're preparing your mind and body for a battle because what you want is so far from where you're at, I recommend both exercises. The more you do to set your mind on the path of success, the more likely you are to achieve the results you want.

If the marriage you have right now is heading down the path to divorce, I highly recommend seeking out a counselor to talk through the change process with you. You may need help communicating with each other effectively, a skill you will need in order to find the kinds of change you're desiring, even if it's not with your current partner.

PLAN

DETERMINE YOUR ACTION PLAN

Now it's time to set a plan in motion to shake some things up in your marriage.

When I knew it was the day to take action, I was so scared to talk to Michael about it. I was afraid of his reaction; I was afraid he would reject me; I was afraid he'd say I wasn't worth the extra effort that I was about to ask him to put in. One way I help calm these kinds of fears is by choosing my timing carefully. Don't talk about it when emotions are heightened. Talk about it when there's not a big blowout hovering just beneath the surface of your relationship.

Make sure you're ready for whatever reaction comes out of your partner's mouth without holding it against them. I've learned that my husband's first reaction to most new information is usually not how he really feels. If I give him some time to process and think, he's usually willing to have a conversation with me pretty quickly. If I don't hold on to what could be a fight, it usually doesn't turn into one.

Let your partner feel what they feel when you start taking action. Change is emotional and it's hard, as we've talked about. Imagine how scared you might feel if your partner came charging into the bedroom talking about all the things that need to change. Be empathetic to them and guide them to resources that might help you both, like books. (This one might be great, even if it's just this section—Hi, spouses! We love you.)

My first few attempts at change in my marriage failed miserably. He was hurt; he didn't understand what I wanted from him; he didn't know my heart because I didn't communicate it. As soon as I met with him and was honest about how I feel now and how I believe a marriage can feel, he started to understand me more. When he understood that I just wanted more of him, it was easier for him to give.

How are you planning to talk to your spouse? What do you want and expect? How can you leave the conversation open for the input from your partner on this? How can you allow them space to process the idea of something more if they've always believed "everything's great!"? What three things are you going to do to move your marriage into a place where you both can feel more fulfilled? What do you commit to change? How can you meet your partner in the middle?

End this step by answering the question, *What three things can you take action on right now that will get you closer to the reality you desire in your life?*

CONNECT PLEASURE AND PAIN

Take the time to do the Fortune 500 and Dickens Process to help you rewire your brain for success. Extra credit to the couple that does both exercises separately and shares the experience afterward. Connect all the pleasure you have and dream of to improving your marriage. Become the person who is capable of that high-level relationship.

GO TO WORK

I did the hundred-day challenge with Michael this year. In April, when I was starting my hundred-days-in-the-gym challenge, I also approached Michael to do one hundred days of sex with me. He will tell you that it scared him. *Can we do that? That's a lot of work. Can I keep up? Will this cause problems?* But he said yes, reluctantly, and yet with high hopes for us. If we failed to keep up, how would that challenge have hurt us? It will either reveal something to work on or it's going to be an amazing experience.

And guys, it was an amazing experience. Today we reached day 371 of sex *every day—bow chicka wow wow*. Over a year at this point and I can feel the difference in every part of our marriage and relationship. We have made sex a priority and a part of our day. It has now become what we do. Some nights when it's late and we've had a hard day, we both have to pull the energy to connect this way out of thin air. It doesn't always feel like what I want to do before we start, but I have never, not once, regretted taking the time in my day to connect with him in the way I don't connect with anyone else in the world. What we have is sacred and special; it's good for us to show up for that.

Ladies and gents, I sense you may have some logistical questions about this challenge. (I get a lot of questions about the idea of sex every day, so you're not alone.) I tried to get the answers slipped into this book without my publisher noticing, but in the end, they were just too taboo to answer in the written word. Find my podcast online (www.lindsaytm. com for links) about the hundred-days-of-sex challenge and I promise to answer your taboo questions with honest answers.[2]

This hundred-day challenge has changed our marriage relationship for the better. Each day, even the days we struggle together, we fight to connect through sex. It's been amazing to see what this simple act has produced for us, and I cannot recommend it highly enough. In the last six months of sex, Michael has learned my body better. I have learned his. We know each other in this intimate way that no other person on the planet does, and that feels amazing. Our sex has become playful and fun and something we look forward to.

It was an entire year before Michael and I had the breakthrough our marriage needed. A year of talking about our feelings, trying to connect when one of us was distant, and adjusting our expectations of what it *should* look like. What I really think is that we were just getting to know each other through change. We just rolled with the ups and downs. It didn't always feel secure; it was the least secure I've ever felt in my marriage, actually. It was darkest before the dawn. November, December, and January felt like the end before it felt like a beginning. Don't panic.

Ride the waves of emotions knowing, without a doubt, that emotions are temporary and they will not last. Always remember they will not last, because your mind will try to convince you otherwise. Your mind is so full of it sometimes. Let the time come and go. Your marriage is worth the effort. This shift for Michael and me has turned into one of the biggest blessings in my life. It has helped me in absolutely every other part of my life. Having a partner who is behind me and supporting me—the real me, flaws and all—has improved my work, my health, my friendships, my finances, and my spiritual connection to God.

The value is here for a good marriage. We all deserve a marriage that makes us feel personal power in the rest of our lives. I have that now. I know that no matter what I choose to work on in my life, I have a partner in my corner who is not only going to support it, but he's also going to push me. He's going to require it from me because he knows my potential and we've built a plan for our lives together. We pursue each other not because we need each other but because we choose each other. Over and over, we choose each other.

Warning: Let me just lay down a disclaimer here when it comes to relationships. If your relationship is abusive in any way, I want you to really consider the threshold for success with the other person. The problem with setting goals in motion when it comes to relationships is that it requires the consent of the other person in the relationship. If the other person isn't capable of the relationship you know you can achieve in your life, it may be time to really think about if this is the right person for this vision. An abusive spouse has no place in your fulfillment. Let me say this again: if you are being abused, you will not find fulfillment there.

You cannot allow someone to physically or emotionally hurt you over and over and expect that you'll be able to ignore it. You don't need to ignore it, and you should not ignore it. Abuse is a hard no for me, and it should be for you. Do not allow someone to manipulate you or the people you love. I have never and will never advocate to keep a relationship together that has experienced abuse. This exercise isn't intended to put a Band-Aid on abuse or to encourage you to stay in a marriage that cannot work for both of you. If that is the case, this is your sign: get the hell out of there. You do not have to stay in an abusive relationship. I love you. You can do this.

FAMILY

Family relationships are perhaps the most complicated of all the relationships. There's so much to contend with when it comes to how families connect, communicate, and grow together. It makes sense that the people you've known the longest will know the most versions of you. Often families will hang on to one version of you, even if you're no longer that person, and they'll try to pin that on you each time they see you. You can do so much growing and changing outside of your family get-togethers, and then it can feel like you're right back to that hurt little child when you get around your family. They bring it out in you, right? We do that to the members of our family too.

Change is hard and families aren't generally open to big changes. It messes up the family dynamics, it doesn't feel safe, and it's uncomfortable. See, there's that word again, uncomfortable. We avoid it at all costs. It may take time to prove to your family that you've changed if you were the person who was constantly the "problem" in the family.

Complications are why family dynamics require an extra dose of communication. There is an unwritten blood-is-thicker-than-water rule when it comes to family. Often that idea makes distancing yourself from behaviors or mindsets that no longer serve you difficult. And that's okay. Remember, just because something is hard doesn't mean it's bad.

EXTENDED FAMILY

How can you avoid the aunt who constantly has something to say about your weight? How do you communicate with the person at family get-togethers who just loves to stir the pot? How do you get to enjoy time with the part of the family that supports you and avoid the ones who don't? We don't always have a say when it comes to family get-togethers. Or do we?

You absolutely do have a say. Your ability to keep your boundaries with family is as easy as figuring out what those boundaries are and then communicating them clearly. You get to choose the behavior you're willing to accept and what you're not.

Boundaries around family can seem really harsh; I realize that. Saying, "I'm not going to allow this kind of behavior in my life or the life of my family" is going to cause a whole scene. That doesn't mean it's wrong. You get to choose the relationships you allow in your life, and just because someone is related to you doesn't mean you're required to see them and put yourself in danger in any way.

I forgave my father long ago for the hurts he gave me. His actions during my childhood weren't about me, they were about him trying to get his highest needs met. I can understand that now as a functioning adult, while I couldn't as a child. I've forgiven him for his decisions as a father that wounded me, but I have chosen to keep a boundary around myself and my family when it comes to him.

Although I'll always have love for my father in a way, I choose to spend my time and effort on the parts of my family that share values with me. I choose to focus the time I would spend with extended family on my children, and you're going to be hard-pressed to convince me that's not the best choice for my personal fulfillment and happiness. It's a boundary that I've placed and one that I will keep firmly in place until I feel the time is right.

> You get to choose the relationships you allow in your life, and just because someone is related to you doesn't mean you're required to see them and put yourself in danger in any way.

Do you have a few families in your life that you look up to? These families are great sources for inspiration on what you'd like your extended-family relationships to feel like. You have the power to create and carry out a plan for a family relationship that actually works. You don't have to tolerate relationships built on shame or pressure. You don't need to accept the kind of relationship that only works for one person while the other just sucks it up. No, you can choose a relationship with your family that feels how you want it to feel.

CHILDREN

I want to have a relationship with my daughters that is built on trust, honesty, and dedication to one another. I don't have a road map for that kind of thing because that's not the environment my family grew up in. So that means I'm relying on what I've seen others accomplish to show me what's possible, to give me a glimpse of what family fulfillment could feel like. Whatever kind of relationship you want with your kids you can have if you put your mind to it. You can have a long-lasting relationship with your kids that feels totally different than it did when you were growing up; you just have to conceive it, believe it can happen, and then go to work putting that plan in action.

I take the time to tell my girls that I want to be their friend one day but that I'm not that right now. I treat them with respect now so that respect is a part of the relationship we have in the future. I answer their questions honestly when they ask them about almost everything (with some exceptions around the things that eleven- and nine-year-olds aren't ready to process yet). I try to tell them all the ways I screwed up when I was younger. I tell them about my relationship with my parents. I share with them who I truly am now so that when they become adults, they don't have to discover me. I've always just been.

I want my three daughters to know me, flaws and all, because so many kids start out believing their parents are perfect and have all the answers. That perception never lasts. I don't want it to be a part of our connection.

Someday, I imagine trips with my girls. I imagine sitting in quaint little towns all over the world, sipping wine and laughing together. I imagine what their kids will look like and how our holidays will look. I have a vision in mind for the relationship I want with my kids and the relationship I want them to have with their dad. I think about it, dwell on it, and put it into action now and every day.

It's time to WOOP your family relationships and think about what you want out of your time with them. Feel free to make this work in your relationships within your own family, extended family, or even your chosen family if they're important in your life.

THE FAMILY WOOP EXPERIENCE

WISH

CONTEMPLATE YOUR DEATH

What kind of impact do you want to have had on your family before your time is up? What if you died today? What would your family be saying and thinking about you? How would they feel about the relationship they had with you? Sit in the feeling of watching your family mourn you. What would you regret if your time was up today?

DESIRE CHANGE

What do you wish your family relationships looked and felt like? How do you want to spend time with your kids once they're out of your house? If they're already gone, what plan do you have to connect with them more often? What kind of relationship do you want to have with your extended family? How often do you want to see them? What kinds of things do you want to do with your family? When your extended family comes around, what kinds of boundaries do you need to set? What's the best way to get to know the people in your family on a personal level? What kinds of relationships do you want to have with your children as they grow and when they become adults? What are your goals for your family? What traditions are important to you when it comes to family? How can you make sure there's an equitable exchange with your family members? How will you show your family that you love them and that they're an important part of your fulfilled life?

Think about what you'd wish for in a family so we can set a plan in motion to bring that very thing to you. Don't wish for something for your family that you know isn't possible, like parents getting back together or people making the decisions *you* want them to make. Figure out what a fulfilling relationship would feel like and be like with the members of your family who are important to you and affect your life.

OUTCOME

THINK FROM A SPIRITUAL PERSPECTIVE

What is your heart longing for when it comes to the relationships with your family? How do you want to connect with your family? How do you want to connect with your children? What kind of relationship are you drawn to with your family? Don't ignore the heartstring tugs your spirit gives you. They're pointing you toward a fulfillment that feels unlike any other.

CONNECT WITH YOUR VALUES

Connect your family relationships to your core values, then figure out what a strong family relationship will do to help you live in a way that is within those values. If you value achievement, find something you can do as a family to achieve, like volunteering a certain number of hours each month. If you value stimulation, create family game nights or dinner traditions that you can do once a week.

OBSTACLE

You know your family dynamics and how it feels to be a part of them. This is the part of the WOOP experience where you list the things that might derail the desires and plans you have for family fulfillment. Think about the things that keep you from being the kind of parent, sibling, son, or daughter you desire to be. Be ready to list the distractions in your life or the lives of your kids that might keep you from connecting the way you want; entertainment comes to mind right away.

What kinds of things threaten to put a stop to your fulfillment with them?

What might your family say when you start pushing for a different, stronger, and more personal relationship with them?

Are there hard conversations you need to have?

Are there apologies you owe?

Are there secrets being kept from family that need to be in the light?

To be prepared to fight for your fulfillment, you have to know what you're up against, and this section will help you be aware of obstacles so you don't quit trying when things get tough.

PLAN

DETERMINE YOUR ACTION PLAN

Create action items that you will dedicate your time and energy to completing. A lot of these kinds of plans have to do with dedicating time and communicating properly with other members of your family. Don't forget that a counselor or therapist can be an amazing tool to help you understand your family members a bit better and how to communicate your desires to them. It is my guess that your kids, cousins, or parents will be excited that you're making the relationship with them a priority in your life. Go get the kind of family relationships you want in your life. Go have the kinds of experiences with the people in your family that make you feel fulfilled when you're with them. You don't have to settle for just okay or partial transparency. You can choose the kind of relationship you'd like to have, one where you don't have to hide parts of you, even if it's never been a reality before.

As mentioned, I'm focused on having an honest and authentic relationship with my kids. I want them to see me and know me because I believe that's the best way to encourage them to let me see them and know them in the same way. For me that means answering their questions without judgment or lies. It means being honest when I make mistakes and apologizing, something I rarely heard as a child. It means letting them see behind the curtain sometimes, even when it's messy back there. I want my kids to know imperfection isn't disqualification, and that comes through letting them see the flaws, mistakes, dumb decisions, and baggage I might have hidden from them at one point in my life. What you wish for, you will have to become. Be prepared for that reality.

Ask yourself the question, *What three things can I take action on right now that will get me closer to the reality I desire in this area?*

> I want my kids to know imperfection isn't disqualification, and that comes through letting them see the flaws, mistakes, dumb decisions, and baggage I might have hidden from them at one point in my life.

CONNECT PLEASURE AND PAIN

Link pleasure and pain to your family relationships. Do the Fortune 500 exercise and the Dickens Process to get your brain on the right path to family fulfillment. Write out all the ways that a fulfilling family life will affect you in all other areas of your life. Give yourself enough leverage to really push the boundaries of what you believe is possible.

If you're a parent, be aware that your children are built-in motivators. If the change you want will have a positive outcome for your children, you will likely stop at nothing to make it happen. Make sure it's realistic and that you're keeping your present duties as a parent in mind. It's not always the right time to be besties with your kids (especially if they're young). Your plan can be slow moving. You can create a road map to transition your relationship with your kids from parent to friend, but it won't and probably shouldn't happen overnight.

GO TO WORK

What kind of fun thing can you think of to do with your kids every day for one hundred days that will be memorable and bring you a closer relationship? What about with other members of your family? The best way to make an action stick is to be consistent about it. Maybe you connect on the phone each day; maybe you play a quick game and keep score for one hundred days; maybe you write each other emails or in a journal you pass back and forth. After one hundred days, I think you'll be shocked by how much has changed in the relationship. All you have to do is try. The result will either be a learning experience or a path to a new relationship. Either way, fulfillment is the destination.

If your family members are reluctant to sign on for one hundred days, think of some simple things you can do without them even knowing it that might build great habits. Perhaps a ten-second hug a day is something you do with your kids. Maybe you write a little note of encouragement every day. Maybe you make a conscious effort to use positive language every day to help cut down on the yelling and fighting. Maybe you write in your journal every day about your family. You can always do the work even if you have a teenager who wants to be one hundred miles away from you. That doesn't mean you'll always get the outcome you want, but it does mean that your family will very likely know you're trying and you actually care about the relationship.

YOUR SPIRIT IS
BEGGING YOU TO
MAKE
YOURSELF
A
PRIORITY

SPIRITUAL FULFILLMENT

I ended with spiritual fulfillment because it's the one that I have changed through the most. I think we can all agree that 2020 was hard in a lot of ways. I'm so grateful for that year in my life, though, because the difficulty and challenge molded me into a spiritual warrior. I'm not talking about a religious warrior. I'm talking about connecting with my spirit and my creator in a way I've never felt in my life. Having those moments where all you can do is hit your knees and pray has made me feel different inside. There's a knowing that I'm loved and protected that wasn't there before. There's an understanding of how things work for my good that wasn't there before. There's a curiosity there that wasn't there before 2020. And I have been to church; I've been to the camps; I did the religion thing. None of that made me feel as free as redefining what I believe to be true about who I was made to be by God.

When I was a little girl around six or seven years old, my parents sent me to a camp of some sort. I knew no one. I remember feeling so alone and not prepared to advocate for myself. I was scared of a lot of things as a little girl. I felt unsafe a good deal of the time, especially alone. The minute I hit the ground at this camp, I perceived it to be an unsafe situation, and it was really uncomfortable. I didn't tell my parents.

I had a panic attack one night and fell asleep alone in a cabin with other girls all around me in their beds. I remember crying and having to work to breathe, which filled me with shame and fear. The camp counselor told my mom that I was "filled with the Holy Spirit," which is apparently another word for panic at that camp, and I believed them. I had no category for what had happened to me, so I believed the adults in the room. My parents never spoke about it with me. I don't blame them; my dad probably didn't know I had a negative experience, and my mom was likely not capable of dealing with that level of emotion at that time in her life.

But that night? That night I realized who I was.

All alone in that bunk bed, fighting for breath and begging for God to fix it, I realized I was a fighter.

I didn't sit around lamenting about this situation my entire life as if it were some kind of trauma. I remember it but I wasn't traumatized by it. I was empowered that night.

Fast forward thirty-four years or so: last month I had another panic attack after my daughters came to me to talk about standing up to someone bullying an animal. I was filled with gratitude that I had daughters willing to stand up for what they believe in at a young age and communicate it as I could not or would not at their age. I started to feel my heart beat faster and faster. At first I thought, *How strange that I'm getting so excited about this sad story my daughters are telling me, but I'm glad they're confident enough to advocate for themselves and others. They're actually telling me they're standing up for what's right, and they have a voice!* And then suddenly, out of nowhere, I felt my fight-or-flight reflex kick in so strongly that I left the room where we were talking and called for my husband. I don't know what set me into a panic; I think it's like that sometimes, which is why understanding your mind can be so difficult.

For hours, literal hours, I paced around the room, laid down all over the place, fought to breathe, puked, cried, shook uncontrollably, apologized, processed my thoughts, and looked for a way to calm my body and mind. In an attempt to ground me, Michael laid with his entire body on top of mine, heart to heart. I love that man for being there for every second of that experience without judgment. This is the true meaning of partnership. He cleaned up my puke and then he laid on top of me while I cried for what felt like ever.

Finally, my heart started to calm, and my breath started to slow. And I started to cry. Really cry. So hard I began to wonder when the last time I cried like that was. It wasn't when my mom died. It wasn't over break-ups. It wasn't when my babies were born. I worked backward through the calendar of my life until I came to that night at camp.

This was the first panic attack I had ever experienced in my adult life, and that event (as terrifying and out of character for me as it was) led me back to that experience as a little girl. I remembered that little girl at that camp. I remembered crying so hard I felt embarrassed. This was familiar. I had been here before. I felt that little girl again. She was there in every breath that I struggled to take. She was in the way I held back the tears at first. She was in the way I felt shame. She was in the way I tried to talk my mind out of survival mode. Little Lindsay was in there reminding me of who I am: *You're safe, you're strong, you're doing it.* And when I let the tears come, they came with fury and vengeance for all the tears I never let myself cry since that night at that camp.

At that moment I realized that the storm that I experienced that night as a little girl wasn't meant to disrupt my life, it was meant to teach me—at age forty. It was meant to remind me of the kind of parent I wanted to be as I remembered thinking to myself, *I'd never leave my kids here alone.* I never wanted to be the mom who's not capable of talking honestly and often about how we feel because I struggled to be honest with my parents about feelings. I wanted to be the kind of mom whose kids would come and talk to about anything big or little. And they did! The things I set into my mind as a child became real as an adult because of that night at that camp.

This experience was here to remind me to let others take care of me. For the first couple of hours as Michael tried to tend to me and keep me breathing, I apologized at least 735 times. I don't want to have to be taken care of; *That's not who I am*, I thought. Did I mention it was the night of his grandfather's funeral? That wrecked me. What kind of wife pulls this shit for her husband to deal with on this night? And I was so wrong to think that way. I do need to be taken care of. I need to be the vulnerable one sometimes. I do need to let my husband see me completely undone. This experience was meant to show me that I can be vulnerable with my emotions, fears, and feelings with my husband as I cried tears that had waited for decades to be released. All it has done is make us more connected. I needed to remember that I wasn't that little girl alone in a cabin any longer. I had to expel her from my body.

This experience was here to remind me that I feel things. I'm a naturally open and empathetic person who had hidden that away out of fear and self-preservation. I'm not that helpless little girl anymore. I'm Lindsay Teague Moreno. I laugh in the face of fear. I stand up and look shame in the eye. I do what my gut tells me no matter what others think. I don't play when it comes to living a life that is meaningful, and I know that's because I discovered her when I was little.

I could go on for an entire chapter about what I remembered that night. What an amazingly horrible, beautiful, broken, and perfect experience. I'm so grateful to have learned that lesson in the way I did. I'm so grateful it was regifted to me at this time in my life.

I believe that night was a God-breathed moment. He set me up for this years ago, and He let me experience every part of it knowing I would come out changed. Since that day, He and I haven't had the same relationship. We understand each other better. I can see His plan. I feel spiritually connected to the divine right now because of this experience.

Have you ever had one of those types of out-of-body experiences where you just know God is behind it? Have the hairs on your body stood up as you saw with fresh eyes something that was so challenging just hours or minutes before? Have you felt emotional out of pure gratitude for the life you've been given and have the opportunity to live out here on earth?

The God who was presented to me at that camp and in my childhood is not the God I know now. He's not the God of rules who can't wait to smite me. He's not ashamed of me. He's not waiting to punish me here on earth for the things that I do wrong. I do plenty of that on my own, and He knows it. I am loved. I know in my mind, body, soul, and spirit that you and I were made of pure love and given the gift of consciousness on purpose. God is in us. We just have to accept that gift and go out searching.

Here's the takeaway: as tough as your storm feels right now, it's shaping you into something new—someone more capable, more wholehearted, more empathetic, more prepared to fulfill your purpose. Start viewing your challenges as future opportunities and it changes everything. God is preparing to use your story for something else entirely. You just have to seek it out.

This year, I've intentionally been seeking out my spiritual connection to God. I want to know why He created me. What am I here for? How can I reach my potential? How can I be used in a greater story than mine?

Simply asking the questions and sitting quietly for the answers has blown my mind. I've been shown things this year through prayer and meditation that I cannot explain. I have an inner peace about the other parts of my life because of the progress I've made in this part of my life. I'm seeing things so much more clearly when I tap into my spirit and allow God to speak into my life. I tend to be loud and big and take up a lot of space in the world. That's who God created me to be, but I have to intentionally quiet myself and prepare to hear the still, small voice. I have to make myself open for the people I know in my life to speak into me and talk to me about what they're hearing.

In the pursuit of God, I surely did find Him, just as is said in the

> As tough as your storm feels right now, it's shaping you into something new— someone more capable, more wholehearted, more empathetic, more prepared to fulfill your purpose.

Bible. I'm not drawn to traditional church right now because I don't want a traditional relationship with God. I want one where we laugh at each other and spend time together because it feels so good.

There's a reason that you're here in this exact moment on earth. You have a purpose, and finding that purpose is a spiritual journey. It's not hiding behind a job; it's not hiding behind the perfect relationship; it's not hiding behind a smaller body or another child. The answer to your purpose is in your spirit, and you'll know it when you feel it. I feel it show up in goosebumps and little signs all over the place. I feel it show up in my gut. I feel it show up in an inner peace when things are falling apart around me. Everything is spiritual: the dirt on the ground, the clouds in the sky, the people you love, the talents and gifts that you have, and the things you believe to be true.

Unleashing your inner spiritual warrior is understanding without a doubt that you were put here for a reason and that you can trust yourself to discover it. In my experience, spirituality comes with a good amount of wrestling with what it is that I believe versus what was taught to me because I grew up in the church and little kids believe what their parents tell them to, for the most part. It may have you questioning your sanity on some days, as I did when I started feeling vibrations all around me. I can feel it. There are times when I can actually observe myself speak words that aren't mine; they're divinely placed into my mouth.

> There's a reason that you're here in this exact moment on earth. You have a purpose, and finding that purpose is a spiritual journey.

I can imagine this all feels really woo-woo, and I can understand that feeling. I've been there, thought that. The thing that really opened up the spiritual gates for me to feel something new in my heart about being alive right now was a combination of curiosity and trusting what I experience. In the past I've been out of touch with my body, meaning I don't hear my body's signals very loud. Take eating, for example; I have struggled to hear the "I'm full now, you can stop eating" signal, which led me to overeating out of ignorance to the signs my body was trying to give me. I ignore pain a lot. Sometimes I just get busy and tune out the signals for a while. I found the same to be true with my spiritual signals. When I'd see a sign or a little coincidence, I'd ignore it or not pay attention to it. I wasn't curious about what those little feelings or signs could mean for me or what they might be trying to tell me.

As I was on a journey toward whole-life fulfillment, I decided to try to become spiritually aware. Here we are again at awareness. I wanted to hear the signals and signs my body, mind, soul, and spirit were giving me. I became curious about what it would feel like if I stopped believing in coincidences altogether. I decided to get my lazy butt out of bed early in the mornings to spend time in meditation/prayer and journaling. I decided to really try to discover God in me and all around me. I started asking for and looking for signs absolutely everywhere. And do you know what I got when I started asking and looking? Exactly what I wanted.

I've been seeking theology experts, gurus, rabbis, priests, pastors, light workers, and enlightened people to help guide me. I have started to trust my "knower" (the part of you that knows if something is correct for you or not) as I sift through what I'm learning and keep what resonates and leave the rest. I've opened myself up to a new kind of relationship with my creator that is with me twenty-four hours a day, seven days a week for my entire life—I just never tried to feel it before with any consistency or passion. And just like I mentioned before, one thing I know about God is that I don't know God. I can't put spirituality in a box because there isn't a box big enough for everything. I can feel that the same life force that is in me is in absolutely everything in the universe, and all of it is touched by the divine.

And there is a peace in that—a peace that passes understanding, just like I learned in vacation Bible school when I was a little girl. There is a calmness in knowing I was chosen, picked out, and created out of infinite possibilities to be on the earth right now and be alive. You were chosen too. Isn't it time we figure out why before we look back and realize we missed the point? What's the good in being wealthy if you don't know how you should use it for your greatest good—something that lasts beyond this life? What's the good in having great relation-

Spirituality gives a deepness and a realness to everything you do.

ships if you can't connect on a profound spiritual level where you can feel each other without saying a word? Spirituality gives a deepness and a realness to everything you do. Your purpose is hiding here if you haven't discovered it yet.

I'm going to go through a WOOP experience with you now. I'm probably not going to give too many specifics on your belief system because that's not my job.

I'm here to guide you to what you believe, not tell you what to believe. I want to be sure that no matter what you believe about how you came to be alive on this planet at this exact moment, you pull value from this section, because spiritual fulfillment is perhaps the most important one.

WISH

CONTEMPLATE YOUR DEATH

This will perhaps be the most palpable of the six cornerstones as you think about death because our spirituality connects to what we believe happens after death here on earth. Maybe you believe that's all there is; that's okay. I'm starting to open up to the idea that our time here on earth is really to serve our higher purpose in the afterlife.

It's okay if you don't come up with the answers right away about how it will feel spiritually at the moment of your death. That's going to be a surprise for all of us. Perhaps it's better to think of how connecting spiritually with your creator will create certainty, even in death. How would you feel if you were given two months left to live and you realized you never took your spirituality seriously?

DESIRE CHANGE

Here's where you decide not to let your life pass you by and feel the sting of regret by putting your spiritual fulfillment on the back burner. Is there a curiosity in you? Maybe you have avoided thinking about the bigger picture in this life and the afterlife because you feel like you don't have or never will have any answers. I've felt that before.

It took me thirty-eight years to decide to look beyond the dogma and doctrine of the modern church to find a connection to God. I figured, *What's the point if He already knows what I'm going to do and how it's going to go in my life?* If you're uninspired spiritually, it's time to start seeking a change in this area.

How do you wish you felt in your soul about the purpose in your life? How would you feel if you woke up every day ready for the surprises and little signs that are waiting for you everywhere you look? What if you could put down what you've been told and believe what feels right in your heart? What if spirituality was more than Sunday mornings and a 10 percent expense in the form of tithing? What if God became real to you? What if you could hear and speak in a divine voice? What might you be missing in your spiritual life that's needed to create curiosity and faith? Is there more out there? Do you stand firm on what you believe to be true about why you're here and who created you?

OUTCOME

THINK FROM A SPIRITUAL PERSPECTIVE

Do you have a feeling you're meant for more? I do. What kind of spiritual fulfillment is available? What examples do you have about what an awakening of your soul can do for you?

I believe the next few years are going to be years of heart, mind, body, and spirit awakening. I think this is the time where we start to see more clearly and vibrate at a higher frequency, the frequencies of love, acceptance, unity, certainty, hope, and excitement for the future. As a collective group, we're going to do this together, and I don't want you to be blind to what is happening all around you. I think we're going to find new leaders, new definitions of the church, and new ideas about what's possible, and the old way will be washed away for so many of us. Change is coming. I can feel it in my spirit.

How will setting your soul on fire for your life impact your experience and the experiences of those around you? What do you feel the tug at your heart to explore or become more curious about? Perhaps some time sitting quietly so you can hear what your creator wants to say to you is a good way to understand what you really want in this area.

CONNECT WITH YOUR VALUES

I see spirituality in each of the ten basic values outlined in this book. I believe spirituality brings a fullness to each of those values. For example, if I value security and a sense of belonging, consciously and spiritually connecting with my community can fulfill that desire for me. When I have those deep heart-to-heart, soul-to-soul discussions with a few of my spiritual friends, I leave refreshed, renewed, and ready to take on challenges. That's a spiritual connection to benevolence.

OBSTACLE

So what's standing in your way?

Let me tell you what held me back for so long: the idea of right and wrong / good and bad. These concepts were drilled into me as a child. I became conditioned to see things through that "spiritual" lens. But those kinds of rules don't feel very spiritual to me. I think our sense of right and wrong should come from inside us. We should feel things out, try things on, see how it affects the way we do life, and then determine if it's right or wrong for us. The religious rules I grew up with kept me afraid of anything that might be connected to New-Age thinking.

As an adult I continued to believe that as well. It wasn't until I intentionally dismantled my beliefs about who God is and what He wants for me that I began to have true faith. It was then that I started seeing God as so much bigger than the size my church had painted Him to be. I was able to feel a divine presence inside my body when I stopped cutting myself off from what I had been taught wasn't godly.

God asks us to wrestle with Him. He asks us to test Him. I believe He wants us to seek Him. And that may not look like you learned in children's ministry or kids' church. It may not look like another Bible story. It may look a lot more like journaling and meditating and looking for signs you're on the right track. And it may lead you right back to church so you can be filled each week by a community of people who love you.

> God asks us to wrestle with Him. He asks us to test Him. I believe He wants us to seek Him.

Perhaps your religious standard operating behavior has become an obstacle for you. What else may stand in your way of finding God in your life? Are you ready to put the time and effort in? Are you worried about what other people think? Because I was. Are you worried you'll get off on the wrong path? Because I was. Have you thought about how it might change your relationships? Take some time to journal the things that are pulling you away from exploring what it means to be truly spiritual.

PLAN

DETERMINE YOUR ACTION PLAN

Make an action plan of things you might want to explore, books you might want to read, podcasts you may be interested in listening to, and other ways to learn about spirituality. If you need help figuring out which actions to take when, feel free to use the tools we've discussed: journaling, meditation, and even drawing it in picture form will help you answer the question, *What three things can I do right now to get me closer to my desired reality?*

I can't recommend highly enough finding someone who has walked this path before you to ask questions of. I have a group of friends who are further along on this road that I constantly ask questions. These kinds of discussions create lasting relationships and an understanding that you're not alone. You aren't the first and you won't be the last to create a plan for enlightenment or to commune with your creator. There are others out there if you search for them.

CONNECT PLEASURE AND PAIN

Take the time to do the Fortune 500 exercise for spiritual development. There is something so powerful about giving yourself the leverage you need to get to work. Don't work against your psychology; use it to help seal your desire for spiritual fulfillment into your mind and it will go to work to find it.

If you really want to give yourself some get-up-and-go on this journey, consider completing the Dickens Process. This will walk you through your life without a spiritual awakening at all. What will it feel like? How will you feel when you're looking at the grave and you're not sure where you go from here? What kind of fullness will you miss in life if you never take the time to seek spiritual fulfillment?

GO TO WORK

Now it's time for some action. What kind of small steps can you make every day that will help you discover spiritual fulfillment in your life? What small thing can you do every day that will at least keep your mind active toward the end goal that you want?

I would suggest finding some guided meditation, maybe some podcasts, or a spiritual leader who could meet with you to help you dig deeper. Can you set aside time to pray at the beginning and end of the day? I find myself falling asleep when I pray at night, and I used to have a lot of shame around that until I was asked by a friend how I feel as a mom when my child falls asleep talking to me about something important to her. What a tender moment. There's no wrong way to get to work on this. Pray about it. Meditate on it.

And then set out to make yourself a spiritual warrior who walks with confidence through every part of your life knowing nothing can split your spiritual connection to your creator. That's your divine right, and I believe it's what God wants from us.

CONCLUSION

A NOTE TO YOU, IN A CHANGING WORLD

I get it. There's all this change for you to make happen and you may be wondering how to apply what you've read in a world that feels like it's racing through the orbits of change too rapidly to grasp. You may be trying to find firm footing and here comes this wake-up call. Whether it's a pandemic, a full quarantine, or all the other things happening in the world from cancel culture to politics, the truth is you can change no matter what. (You're actually changing now, even if you didn't opt in to it.) It's actually easier to change while everything else is morphing into different forms because there's less resistance. My message to you is the same: wake up and commit to the change.

Don't wait until it gets "better" or "things go back to normal." Don't wait until the stars align. Don't wait until you lose something so precious to you that you're forced into it. Don't wait until you have the support of everyone you know. Things won't go back to their former state, and you don't really want them to, if you're doing the right work to change. The past wouldn't fit you anymore anyway. Even though things around you may feel heavier, put down the weight of the world and just carry your part. Let these six cornerstones of a good life, your values, your goals, and your desires drive you forward. Harness the support you need if you find yourself dealing with hard feels (a counselor and a few supportive humans to walk forward with). Whatever you do, don't let change come and leave you in a state of FOMO because you froze in response to all of the movement around you. Make an agreement with yourself that you will wake up and move with the winds of change, not fight against them. Hold your future with an open hand and a clear mind. You'll never be more ready than you are right this very second.

A NOTE TO YOU, PARENTS

A lot of you are having tough conversations with yourselves that go a little something like this:

"Okay, so if I start prioritizing my personal health and spend time doing the things that will make me happy (business, hobbies, time to use as I want), I'm going to be taking that time away from my family."

Yes. Yes, you are.

My question back to you is, "Why is the thought of your family watching you and accommodating you as you care about your own well-being and needs a negative thing? Don't you do that for them all the time?"

It is not selfish to make time for yourself *every single day*. You are an equal member of your family. You are not the hired help. Fulfilled parents are amazing, strong beings who provide the best example to their kids of how to live a life that is authentic and serves everyone in the family at the same time—including themselves. If you work outside the home, your absence from your kids during that time each day makes them stronger and more self-disciplined. What if your daughter learned to make herself a priority in her future relationships after your example? What if your son becomes the kind of husband who supports his future spouse as they pursue what they love because he watched you first? How can that be negative?

Put time for you on your calendar and create boundaries around it so you aren't always picked last in the fulfillment lottery. Because an unfulfilled parent creates an unfulfilled family. In order for the family to thrive, everyone has to have the chance to thrive, and that includes us, parents.

A NOTE TO YOU, MY FRIEND

Here's the deal. Creating a vision of the life we'd like to live isn't hard. In fact, it's pretty fun and satisfying. It's easy to see all the problems we have now and say, "If this wasn't a problem, then I'd be happy." But that's just a lie we tell ourselves to keep ourselves safe and warm in the house and story we've built for ourselves.

Yesterday, Michael and I took our kids to see the first Harry Potter movie at our local theater.[1] Don't you just love summer movies that come back to theaters? There's a part of that film that punched me right between the eyes, and I want to share it with you because I think we've all been in this situation, and we can see how much harder it really is than we give it credit for.

In the scene when Hagrid, the Hogwarts school gamekeeper, comes to get Harry before his first day of school, he busts down the door to the hut where his aunt and uncle had hidden him away from the world of magic. At that moment, Harry has one story about his life in his head. It's a story he believes. His mom and dad had died when he was little, and he was nothing more than a house slave for his aunt Petunia, uncle Vernon, and cousin Dudley. As a little boy, he was stuck in this story, resigned to a small life of sadness and monotony. He didn't love it, but it was all he knew.

In seconds, Hagrid destroys the story that Harry believed about who he was and what he was capable of when he tells Harry that he's not only a wizard but one of the best and most powerful wizards ever born.

Harry has a choice at that point.

He can leave behind the world he knows (and that has kept him relatively safe) for a new story. A new path. A new future. But to do that, he must burn down the old house. He has to be willing to walk away from what he perceived as comfort before and walk into a new world completely foreign to him. Not only that, but Hagrid is a literal giant with a huge beard, and he looks really scary. Stay or go? Hang on or let go? Make it work or find something new?

In the movie we see Harry as a brave and powerful boy who made the choice to write a new story about his life. But I challenge you to think about how difficult it would actually be to make a choice like that. How many people do you know who believe a story that's been told to them about their own lives so they stay "stuck" in it, because leaving that story means facing too much unknown and too many fears? Many domestic abuse stories that end with the woman back in the house of her abuser with another excuse as to why she has two black eyes are just that.

We cling to our old story because we think we're safe there. Even if we're not physically safe, at least we aren't dead, or at least we still have the comforts of home. Nobody expects anything from us there—especially not ourselves. Most of us believe the story we were originally told about who we are, and we never take the time to uncover a new story because the fear is too loud.

This is a problem.

Fear is loud. It's so loud. That's especially true when we dare challenge the narrative that keeps us small and subservient. At least we get fed when we're small and needy. At least we aren't expected to produce any results. At least nobody is depending on us whom we might let down. At least nobody knows the things we've done and the choices we've made in the past if we don't make any noise. We'll just stay here in this story, and we'll be grateful for it. In fact, we'll convince ourselves we like it, and we want to stay here in this house of lies.

Screw that. No, you do not.

If you do, you'll be completely ignorant to the story you could write about who you are and what you're capable of achieving in your life. There's something special in you, but you have to believe it for yourself first. Nobody can do that kind of work for you. You have to admit that there's another level here—that there's more out there for you if you would only open yourself up to the possibility.

You can change your life. You can. You just have to decide that what's in front of you is worth what you're holding on to so tightly.

When you release that tight grip, you will have all of these tools in your hand, ready to help you create something new, ready to help you live the life of your dreams while you're wide awake.

Are you ready to believe that there's another story out there for you?

Are you willing to start exploring what that kind of life might look and feel like?

Do you hear that? The rooster is crowing again. That's your signal to wake up!

It's time.

I'm in your corner. I'm rooting you on. Listen for me cheering for you. My voice is in that crowd.

I love you and I can't wait to see you wake up to the life you were created for.

XO,

LTM

ACKNOWLEDGMENTS

This book wouldn't be possible without the following:

1. An idea placed in me that I couldn't escape, that's what I call a God thing, and I'm done running from them. Bring on the next terrifying idea. I'm all-in.

2. My supportive husband and the manager of my writing career, Michael Moreno. He loves me, and I love him, and together we have built a life that neither of us wants to be asleep through. I'm so grateful for your partnership, M. I love you. So much. Montana, here we come.

3. My three daughters, Boston, Teagan, and Kennedy, who were willing to sacrifice their time with me for the vision I had for this book. I love you three weirdos. I hope you look back at the time we didn't spend together as I was writing this book and remember to make time in your lives to do the things you're called to, even if you have kids of your own. Nah, *because* you have kids of your own.

4. My right hand for the last seven years, Elizabeth Bienas. For real, though, I wouldn't know where my right hand was if it wasn't for you. You are a rare breed, Liz. You roll with whatever I throw at you, and you're always willing to try with me, even when we have

no business trying. Thanks for all of the five-minute reminders and then laughing with me when I inevitably forget.

5. Someone to pray for me on my behalf, encourage me when the fear started to take over, and send me songs to make my day. That's you, Yoshika Green. You are a gem of a human being, and I'm so proud to have your hand in this book. Thank you for teaching me and speaking truth to me. And also? Thanks for being a lover of words with me. Here's more for the book of words: mellifluous, elixir, capitulate.

6. My publishing team: Stephanie Newton, Dawn Hollomon, Caren Wolfe, Damon Reiss, Ashley Reed, Maria Gagliano, and the rest of the W team who fought against the insanity that was 2020 to print this book. I'm proud of the work we did together.

7. My agents, Mike Salisbury and Matt Yates, at Yates & Yates. You guys changed my life. Writing books has been a highlight in my career, and I have you to thank for the chance to write them. Thanks for believing in me and ironing out all the details on my behalf.

8. The select few who took their time to read this book before it hit the shelves (names and endorsements in the front of the book). Thanks for knowing me before this book, and thanks for knowing me after. Most of all, thanks for supporting this kind of work—the kind that's different, a little bit scary, sometimes uncomfortable, and makes you look inside yourself for that next level. This community has had a profound effect on my life. Thank you for pushing, inspiring, and encouraging me.

9. Someone to make words in a book into a work of art: Brad Vetter. How we got you to agree to this project is a mystery to me, but I am so glad we connected over *Wake Up!* I will love the art on and in this book for the rest of my life.

THE *WAKE UP!* CHEAT SHEET FOR LIVING YOUR GOOD LIFE

A re you ready to share what you've learned in *Wake Up!*, but your head is spinning with life-changing ideas? Don't worry. I know the feeling. Here you'll find both book and chapter summaries to help you turn the major concepts into shareable bits of content.

WAKE UP! IN A FEW WORDS

Wake Up! is filled with big ideas and challenges that will change your life if you're ready. Lindsay Teague Moreno tells her story of burning her old life to the ground and finding whole-life fulfillment that will have you questioning everything you think you know, in the very best way. It's the dawn of a new day, and this book is your first step.

WAKE UP! IN A FEW MORE WORDS

Wake Up! is the first step to getting what you truly want out of life. You know your potential, and you've seen glimpses of greatness, but your conditioning is keeping you stuck.

Lindsay Teague Moreno tells her story of waking up and making a choice to live consciously. She's going to teach you how to find whole-life fulfillment, walking you through the deep and scary process with actionable activities.

Do you hear the rooster crowing? It's time to wake up!

CHAPTER 1

You are worthy of living "the good life," but it doesn't come without fighting for change. In chapter 1, Lindsay explains how she achieved whole-life fulfillment by living with six distinct areas of focus called The Cornerstones of a Good Life. She walks you through an exercise to determine how fulfilled you feel today to clarify which areas need work.

CHAPTER 2

If you've spent your life trying to make changes that don't stick, chapter 2 of *Wake Up!* is going to help you understand why. Lindsay explains how automatic behaviors keep you stuck and walks you through an exercise that will shift your perspective. It's time to create new programming that pushes your mind past your previous threshold of success.

CHAPTER 3

Learning about The Four Endowments and The Twelve Universal Laws were integral to Lindsay's change process. The Four Endowments are gifts from God that help us to choose the correct path. The Twelve Universal Laws help reframe your mindset and set yourself free. In chapter 3, she explains these concepts and the significant role they've played in her healing.

CHAPTER 4

Values help you determine what's most important in your life, and fulfillment comes when you work toward the things you value highly. In chapter 4, you will discover or get reacquainted with what those things stand for using the Schwartz theory of basic values. The clarity gained from this exercise creates the foundation for meeting your goals.

CHAPTER 5

In chapter 5, Lindsay walks you through an intensive exercise to get your mind and body to create long-lasting change. The WOOP (wish, outcome, obstacle, plan) framework was developed by Gabriele Oettingen using twenty years of research on motivation. If you put the time into the WOOP experience and commit to immersing yourself in the activity, it will change the way you think.

CHAPTER 6

Personal fulfillment gets a bad rap because society tells us that acting in our own interests is selfish. We've been conditioned to believe that we should think only of the greater good. In chapter 6, readers are shown that personal fulfillment is important because we alone are responsible for our decisions.

CHAPTER 7

In chapter 7, Lindsay debunks the myth of balance through the story of building her first million-dollar business. She explains how it might be necessary to intentionally allow low-priority areas to stand idle while you focus most of your attention on your top priorities. There's no shame in work and business fulfillment.

CHAPTER 8

Society has made money taboo to talk about, but Lindsay isn't here for it. In chapter 8, she explains it's not about the money but about the mindset. You'll see that financial fulfillment doesn't have to be a challenge through the activity in chapter 8.

CHAPTER 9

Women are usually so busy taking care of everyone else, they put off taking care of their health. In chapter 9, Lindsay tells the story of taking control of her health and building lasting habits by shifting her perspective. It's time to ditch the excuses and work on our health fulfillment.

CHAPTER 10

In chapter 10, Lindsay focuses on setting goals in three relationship types: marriage, family, and friendship. Connections and relationships with other people are an integral part of a good life. Lindsay explains how to achieve relationship fulfillment by leaning on your values and having honest conversations with your loved ones.

CHAPTER 11

There's a reason that you're here at this exact moment on earth. You have a purpose, and finding that purpose is a spiritual journey. Lindsay tells a story of a difficult time in her childhood and how it empowered her to seek spiritual fulfillment at age forty. Spirituality gives a realness to everything you do.

NOTES

CHAPTER 1: THE GOOD LIFE

1. Nielsen Total Audience Report: February 2020, page 18, https://www.nielsen.com/us/en/insights/report/2020/the-nielsen-total-audience-report-february-2020/.
2. John P. Robinson, "Americans Less Rushed But No Happier: 1965–2010 Trends in Subjective Time and Happiness," *Social Indicators Research* 113, 1091–1104 (2013), https://doi.org/10.1007/s11205-012-0133-6.
3. Frank Newport, "Snapshot: Average American Predicts Retirement Age of 66," Gallup, https://news.gallup.com/poll/234302/snapshot-americans-project-average-retirement-age.aspx.
4. Sean Dennison, "64% of Americans Aren't Prepared for Retirement—and 48% Don't Care," Global Rankings, September 23, 2019, https://www.gobankingrates.com/retirement/planning/why-americans-will-retire-broke/.
5. John Csiszar, "What a Comfortable Retirement Will Cost You in Each State," Global Rankings, November 6, 2020, https://www.gobankingrates.com/retirement/planning/comfortable-retirement-cost-state/.
6. Kevin Nast, "The Top 10 Reasons Why People May Not Plan for Retirement," NastGroup Financial, August 24, 2015, http://nastgroupfinancial.com/the-top-10-reasons-why-people-may-not-plan-for-retirement/.

CHAPTER 2: THE TIMELINE OF CHANGE

1. Rich Becker, "If 80 Percent of People Won't Change, Why Force Them?" Words. Concepts. Strategies., September 25, 2020, http://www .richardrbecker.com/2014/03/if-80-percent-of-people-wont-change-why. html.

2. Joan MacDonald (@trainwithjoan), Instagram, https://www.instagram .com/trainwithjoan/.

3. Aaron O'Neill, "Life Expectancy (from Birth) in the United States, 1860–2020," Statista, February 3, 2021, https://www.statista.com /statistics/1040079/life-expectancy-united-states-all-time/.

4. Joe Dispenza, "How to Reprogram Your Mind for Success," YouTube, November 4, 2019, https://youtu.be/0u5SU9iDzxg.

5. Joe Dispenza, "The Next Level," Joe Dispenza (blog), September 11, 2020, https://blog.drjoedispenza.com/the-next-level.

CHAPTER 3: THE FOUR ENDOWMENTS AND THE TWELVE UNIVERSAL LAWS

1. Stephen R. Covey, "Four Human Endowments," FranklinCovey, https:// resources.franklincovey.com/blog/four-human-endowments.

2. Sarah Regan, "The 12 Universal Laws and How to Practice Them," MBG Mindfulness (blog), July 21, 2021, https://www.mindbodygreen .com/articles/the-12-universal-laws-and-how-to-practice-them; the laws are often associated with Ho'oponopono, a meditation for freedom originating in ancient Hawaiian culture. Some of the laws, however, are also attributed to hermetic philosophy going back to ancient Egypt.

3. Hermes Trismegistus, *Hermetica*.

4. Darryl Anka, "The Ides of March," 1996, http://www.bashar.org/about /IdesofMarch.html, Internet Archive, capture date April 8, 2000, http:// web.archive.org/web/20000408045421/http://www.bashar.org/about /IdesofMarch.html.

CHAPTER 4: VALUES

1. S. H. Schwartz, "An Overview of the Schwartz Theory of Basic Values," *Online Readings in Psychology and Culture*, Vol. 2, December 1, 2012, https://www.researchgate.net/publication/271231569_An_Overview_of _the_Schwartz_Theory_of_Basic_Values.

CHAPTER 5: THE WOOP EXPERIENCE

1. Gabriele Oettingen, WOOP My Life, https://woopmylife.org/en/.
2. Society for Personality and Social Psychology, "How Thinking about Death Can Lead to a Good Life," ScienceDaily, April 19, 2012, www .sciencedaily.com/releases/2012/04/120419102516.htm.
3. "Americans Place Significant Pressures on Themselves to Reach Life Milestones," H&R Block, July 23, 2019, https://www.hrblock.com /tax-center/newsroom/filing/personal-tax-planning/life-milestones/.
4. Patti Dobrowolski, "Draw Your Future," TEDx Talks, January 10, 2012, https://www.youtube.com/watch?v=zESeeaFDVSw.
5. Kerwin Rae, "How to Stop Falling Back into Old Patterns" (Facebook post), August 1, 2020, https://www.facebook.com/kerwinrae/videos /1193284691029286/.
6. Tony Robbins, "3 Steps to Unlocking Potential," https://www.tonyrobbins .com/personal-growth/unlocking-potential/.
7. Society for Personality and Social Psychology, "How We Form Habits, Change Existing Ones," ScienceDaily, www.sciencedaily.com /releases/2014/08/140808111931.htm.
8. Lindsay Jean Thomson, The 100-Day Project, https://the100dayproject .org/.

CHAPTER 9: HEALTH FULFILLMENT

1. Vera Sizensky, "New Survey: Moms Are Putting Their Health Last," HealthyWomen, March 27, 2015, https://www.healthywomen.org/content /article/new-survey-moms-are-putting-their-health-last.
2. Lindsay Teague Moreno (@lindsayteague), Instagram, July 6, 2020, https://www.instagram.com/p/CCUHlydniwo/.

CHAPTER 10: RELATIONSHIP FULFILLMENT

1. Marco Pereira and Maria Cristina Canavarro, "Relational Contexts in Adjustment to Pregnancy of HIV-Positive Women: Relationships, Social Support and Personal Adjustment," AIDS Care, Vol. 21, Issue 3, 301–308, March 1, 2009, https://doi.org/10.1080/09540120802183453.
2. Lindsay Teague Moreno (@lindsayteague), Instagram, July 9, 2020, https:// www.instagram.com/tv/CCcRARvHWdF/.

ABOUT THE AUTHOR

Lindsay Teague Moreno is a bestselling author, business owner, speaker, and podcaster. In eight years, she's built multiple million-dollar-producing businesses in the retail, direct, and online sales spaces and built a life that works for her rather than the other way around.

Lindsay's love of seeing people level up and live an authentic life has driven her to study values-based fulfillment. When she's not writing, you can find Lindsay perfecting her tree pose, traveling with her family, avoiding any and all chores, or trying to convince her family that a red panda is a perfectly acceptable pet.

Website: https://lindsaytm.com
Instagram: https://instagram.com/lindsayteague
Podcast: https://bossuppodcast.com
Courses: https://learn.lindsaytm.com/courses
100-Day Challenge: https://wakeupbooks.com
Email: hello@lindsaytm.com

MOMTREPRENEURS, LISTEN UP!

You don't have time for another "change everything you're doing on social media and be just like me" book. You need information, and you need it fast. Do you want to grow your following, sell more product, and experience the freedom that comes with being a lady boss?

Getting Noticed isn't the "secret to social media"—it's a no-fluff, take-charge guide to the way we present ourselves, our businesses, and connect with customers online.

Lindsey Teague Moreno knows the hardcore mom life. In between wash cycles, packing lunches, and balancing a to-do list that would make Santa jealous, she grew a business from nothing into a team of 300,000 people producing over $15,000,000 each month in just three years. Lindsay knows you don't have time for another book that leaves you with temporary warm fuzzies but no real content for actually building your business. Getting noticed is the first step to entrepreneurial success in our fast-paced, online world.

Step up your game.

THIS AIN'T YOUR MAMA'S BUSINESS BOOK.

Boss Up! will help you put your business on the map and the ideas you've previously only dreamed about into the marketplace. It will help you overcome your fears and guilt to find a fulfillment that changes you and your family for the better. And it will help you break free of the hard and boring and allow you to have fun along the way.

In *Boss Up!* Lindsay Teague Moreno helps you gain the confidence to know that having ambition doesn't make you a bad mother or wife. That it's okay to have a desire for something more than endless sippy cups, clean-ups, Band-Aids, and groundings. That no matter your education or experience, you can tap into your passions and create businesses that give you increased flexibility, fulfillment, and financial security.

And Lindsay doesn't just do this through commiserating but, instead, through giving you the tools for change. Using the lessons she learned on her own path to success, Lindsay shares real, solid business principles with ten distinct success philosophies that you will encounter on the journey to entrepreneurship, such as:

- Think Long Term
- Be Unapologetically Yourself
- Use the Unsales Tactic
- Understand Your Why
- and many more

Stay-at-home mom turned multimillion-dollar-producing business owner Lindsay Teague Moreno doesn't just have a passion for entrepreneurship. She has a deep passion for helping women from all walks of life gain the confidence and skills to tap into their ambition and achieve success in their own business endeavors.